Sacred
Rosary

An Ignatian Way to Pray the Mysteries

Includes Marian Reflections and Prayers
from St. John XXIII to Pope Francis

Art by

Mary Grace Thul, OP

Foreword Commentary

Reginald Martin, OP & David Keith Townsend, SJ

William M. Watson, SJ

PRAISE FOR SACRED STORY ROSARY

Bill Watson gives us in *Sacred Story Rosary* very original keys to enter into "the experience of the sacred feminine." Through these pages we are introduced to the heart of the Christian mystery in a special way: with Mary's soul that is, the soul of a mother and a woman who "knew how to keep and ponder things in her heart." Also with the heart of Saint Ignatius, as *Sacred Story Rosary* integrates the meditation of the ancient mysteries with the method of Ignatian prayer in which contemplation of each mystery is accomplished in "letting it find me."

Sacred Story Rosary is a beautiful example of how the good practices of the past help us travel the roads of the future.

Javier Melloni, S.J., Th.D.
Author, *The Spiritual Exercises in the Western Spiritual Tradition*

Fr. Watson's book is more than simply the latest reflection on the Mysteries of the Rosary; it is an invitation to enter into the Mysteries in a new way. The genius of St. Ignatius' *Exercises* is the part they play in the larger scheme of one's spiritual life, something an individual traditionally comes to understand under the guidance of a spiritual director.

Fr. Reginald Martin, OP
From the Foreword

This disarmingly small booklet packs a powerful spiritual punch. Father Bill Watson's "Marian Awakening" is nothing short of a wake-up call for anyone whose prayer life has become stale or lukewarm. By offering a practical methodology for effectively praying the Rosary, the author has made this timeless devotion more accessible to everyone. By directing our attention to the Sacred Mysteries imbedded in the stories of each decade of the Rosary, he invites the reader to discover their own personal sacred story in a whole new light. This booklet will change not only the way you pray the Rosary, but how you live your life.

Mary Cunningham Agee,
President and Founder, *The Nurturing Network*

In an admirable and creative manner Bill Watson integrates into the praying of the Rosary the Ignatian suggestions for praying the Scriptures, especially the Gospels (the Preludes and the Points).

David Keith Townsend, S.J.
From the Foreword

Find a quiet corner, take a deep breath, and give yourself over completely to this book. Whether you are a beginner or an experienced practitioner, it will make the experience of the Rosary fresh and deeply personal for you. It will help you focus not on the words or the mechanics of saying the Rosary, but on the true Mystery, ultimately lifting your prayer to a new and more meaningful level.

Barbara Mujica
Author, *Sister Teresa* and *Teresa de Avila, Lettered Woman*

Fr. Bill Watson, S.J. is to be congratulated for his new book, *Sacred Story Rosary*, which explains how to use the Ignatian method of entering into the mysteries of Jesus and Mary. I was struck by the way *Sacred Story Rosary* connects with Saint Pope John Paul II's letter on the Rosary.

In his letter on the Rosary reminds us that every event of Jesus' life is a "mystery" that throws light on the Mystery, which is Christ Himself. The Pope explains that every mystery of Christ brings a "grace," a "saving power," which is given or "released" to us through our participation in the Liturgy and through the "contemplation of those mysteries."

The Rosary is a very practical way on entering into the "mysteries," which otherwise might remain abstract ideas. Do we often think of the Incarnation, the Crucifixion, the Resurrection, the giving of the Spirit, outside of the Rosary? Pope John Paul II recommends "the method of prayer proposed by Saint Ignatius of Loyola" as a way to visualize and to concentrate on the mysteries.

The Pope also suggested "using a suitable icon to portray the mystery ... *to open up a scenario* on which to focus our attention" and Sr. Mary Grace is to be congratulated for her inspiring illustrations of the twenty mysteries, which also lead us to visualize and enter into the mysteries.

Denis Vincent Wiseman, O.P., S.T.D.
Author, *Salvation and Mary in the Writings of Catherine of Sienna*
Theologian, *Tangaza University College Nairobi Kenya*

Father Watson has given us an exciting, new way to pray the Rosary. No more rattling through the beads. Now each mystery can open for us a door to heaven.

Most Reverend George V. Murry, S.J.
Bishop of Youngstown, OH

This little book is contemplative prayer at its practical best. Fr. Bill Watson models *Sacred Story Rosary* after the five-step movement of the *Examen*, the strategic spiritual exercise of St. Ignatius of Loyola. He guides us through each mystery of the rosary by way of a dynamic discipline that primes us to say a wholehearted Yes to our personal share in Christ's mission. Here is a prayer practice that inspires us to be missionary disciples for the new evangelization.

Margaret M. Turek, S.T.D.
Director, *Office of Faith Formation and Evangelization*
Diocese of Oakland, California

Other Books by William Watson, SJ

Sacred Story Affirmations:
Meditations on Discernment of Spirits

Inviting God into Your Life:
A Practical Guide for Prayer

Forty Weeks:
An Ignatian Path to Christ with Sacred Story Prayer

Sacred Story:
An Ignatian Examen for the Third Millennium

Reflections and Homilies:
The Gonzaga Collection

Sacred Story Press
1401 E Jefferson St., STE 405
Seattle, WA 981222

IMPRIMI POTEST
Rev. Scott R. Santarosa, S.J.

IMPRIMATUR
+ George V. Murry, S.J.
Bishop of Youngstown

ISBN-13: 978-1511738040
ISBN-10: 1511738049

Dedicated to Our Lady of the Way

Book cover, layout and design by William M Watson, S.J.

Acknowledgments

It takes many hands and hearts to create a book like this one. I would like to express my sincere gratitude first to Sister Mary Grace Thul, O.P. Mary Grace has been doing religious art, especially art linked to the Mysteries of the Rosary, since the 1960's. In discussion with her for this project, we decided the medium for the images would be collage. I am very pleased with the outcome.

It is a testimony for the Jesuits and Dominicans to be working together on a book dealing with the Rosary. Fortunately, Mary Grace has a brother who is a Jesuit so she has had years of collaborative experience with the Society. Thank you Sister Mary Grace for your inspiration and your faith that is reflective in your works of art. The s special Full Color Collector's Edition of this same book is in honor of your many years of creating beauty to inspire us in our faith.

Special thanks also go to Teresa Lefranc who worked with Fr. Arturo Araujo, S.J., on the translation of this work into Spanish. The Spanish edition, entitled, *Historia Sagrada El Rosario* has the creative genius of Fr. Arturo Araujo whose unique black ink drawings help us enter the Mysteries as powerfully as do those of Sister Mary Grace. My sincere gratitude to each one of you!

THE ROSARY

Is the book of the blind,
where souls see and there enact
the greatest drama of love
the world has ever known.

It is the book of the simple,
which initiates them into mysteries and knowledge
more satisfying than the education of other men.

It is the book of the aged,
whose eyes close upon the shadow of this world,
and open on the substance of the next.

The power of the Rosary is beyond description.

Venerable Fulton J. Sheen

In the Church's traditional spirituality, the veneration of icons
and the many devotions appealing to the senses, as well as the
method of prayer proposed by
Saint Ignatius of Loyola in the Spiritual Exercises,
make use of visual and imaginative elements

(*composition of place*), judged to be of great help
in concentrating the mind on the particular mystery.
This is a methodology, moreover, which corresponds to the
inner logic of the Incarnation:
in Jesus, God wanted to take on human features.
It is through his bodily reality that we are led into contact with
the mystery of his divinity.

St. John Paul II [1]

"The Rosary always accompanies me in my life."[2]

Pope Francis

CONTENTS

AUTHOR'S PREFACE

Dear Friend

On a mid-January day in 1994 I arrived at Drumalis House, the historic Arts and Crafts style manor that would be my home for thirty days. It sat on top of the highest hill in the town of Larne, County Antrim, Northern Ireland, strategically sited so you could see most of the Port of Larne and the Belfast shipyards of Harland and Wolff who built the Titanic. Drumalis House was built by Sir Hugh Smiley in 1873. Smiley owned the Northern Whig Club in Belfast, founded in 1791 by the Society of United Irishmen who were known for their radical politics.

From Smiley's magnificent estate you can still see Harland and Wolff shipyards but also now the Northern Ireland homeport of the P&O Ferry. Their Stranraer, Scotland ferry sailed nine-times daily. I learned its departure times from the bellowing horns that echoed each time it set sail across the strait to Loch Ryan and Stranraer. Since the 1930s, Drumalis House has been run as a retreat center by the Sisters of the Cross and Passion. It was at Drumalis that I and eight other Jesuits from seven different countries, with our Irish and English Jesuit retreat directors, began a Thirty Day Ignatian retreat.

Ever since entering the Society of Jesus, I had a strong devotion to Christ and to the Sacred Heart. I never had a devotion to the Blessed Mother and I never prayed the Rosary—ever! Jesus was my go-to guy for prayer. Yet on this retreat, the Blessed Mother was everywhere: in my prayer, in my dreams and in my daily thoughts. Its unexpectedness was strange, even alarming to me, yet I found myself consoled.

Why would Mary make an appearance now, at this point in my life? I had no idea. All I could venture was this thought: "I know who Jesus is to me, but not Mary. Maybe I am supposed to find out." Over the course of the retreat and up to the present day, Mary's presence in my life has gifted me with an experience of the holy feminine, bringing a new balance to my spirituality and my emotional life.

The experience prompted me to ponder Mary's role for and in the world. I read Marian theology and even acquainted myself with Marian apparitions. But mainly what Mary represents to me are the virtues of humility, simple faith, and trust in God's power and promise.

Twenty years a Jesuit, I had become sophisticated and worldly-wise and a bit removed from simple faith, humility or a belief in miracles. God shocked me on that retreat and many times since out of my arrogant reverie.

Mary taught me the power of her intercession for me in my daily walk with her Son. I was deeply comforted in surrendering to her invitations and discovered from it a simpler faith and trust in God. I discovered too that the majority of people I encounter are responsive to this Marian message of simple faith and trust in the Lord's abiding love.

We all desperately need God's grace in our daily life, in our Church and in our world. What has been unleashed in the world by the original disobedience cannot be matched by human efforts alone. This is why God did not send an army when the time had reached its fulfillment. He sent the Angel Gabriel to a virgin whose humility would open human history to the miraculous power of God.

"My soul proclaims the greatness of the Lord;
My spirit rejoices in God my savior. For he has looked upon his
handmaid's lowliness. Behold, from now on will all ages call me
blessed. He has shown might with his arm, Dispersed the arrogant
of mind and heart. He has thrown down the rulers from their
thrones but lifted up the lowly"
(Lk 1: 46-48, 51-52).

The history of God's work through Mary's docility is a profound lesson for me. God's miraculous strength is something we all need in the face of our personal weaknesses and evil's apparent advantage in the world.

Because of my experience on that retreat, I learned to pray a Rosary nearly every day. It slows me down and focuses my heart on the fundamental mysteries of life. Indeed, I get many inspirations and ideas about my life and the projects in which I am engaged when I pray the Rosary.

The Universal Mysteries of Life

The entrance of Mary into my life happened simultaneously

with my re-discovery of the daily Ignatian *Examen*; a practice I had let slip some years before. I realized the *Examen* encompasses the entire *Spiritual Exercises* in thumbnail. This is why St. Ignatius wanted Jesuits to pray it twice daily. Learning and praying the *Examen* and the Rosary caused them to influence each other and to bleed together in my religious imagination.

As my spiritual life developed over the last twenty years, an important realization dawned for me about the *Examen* and the Rosary's mysteries. The *Examen* emerged as a pathway to the *Sacred Story* of the universe and my own life. And the Rosary's mysteries began to take on universal significance as archetypal truths of the one *Sacred Story* relevant to all people for all time.

There is only one Story in the cosmos that Pope Francis called a Love Story—the Father's work in the Church for the world.[3] When I pray the *Examen*, I am asking for the graces to understand that Love Story, where I am in relation to its ideal, where I have fallen short, and seeking forgiveness, recommitting to its truth. When I pray the Rosary, I also enter into to that same Love Story and contemplate its many unique facets, discovering what God has accomplished and how I am being called to participate in the Greatest Story of all time.

As a Jesuit, I have also been profoundly influenced in my practice of the *Examen* and the Rosary by the special missions given to the Society of Jesus by the popes who have led the church since I entered the Jesuits in August of 1973. Many of my 8-day retreats both before and after my time in Ireland have been spent reading and praying over our Jesuit Constitutions and the documents from our General Congregations that detail those special missions.[4]

In 2008, Pope Benedict XVI missioned the Society of Jesus to address the challenges the Church faces in positively proclaiming Jesus as the Savior of all humanity and the gifts of human nature, family life and human sexuality. We know the salvific mission of Christ entrusted to the Church—the Gospel Kerygma—and the gifts God gave us as human persons endowed by the Holy Spirit to share that Gospel, still pose difficulties, or are even roadblocks to belief for many people.[5]

These papal missions have formed my spiritual imagination and my reflections on the Rosary as much as anything. It is my wish to engage a new generation of faithful to walk with these Universal Mysteries of the cosmos so they see more clearly the glory of human nature and the work Christ has accomplished for all of humanity in our salvation. Each of us needs to center our hearts on what is true and real. Only then, can we with Christ, be the living body—an acceptable sacrifice—capable of responding to the mission of the Church in our age.

I learned a way to pray the Rosary that helps me enter more deeply into the ultimate mysteries of God, humankind and the cosmos. This prayer, along with the *Examen* of St. Ignatius, guides me in my work with the Sacred Story Institute.[6] Whether or not you have discovered *Forty Weeks: An Ignatian Path to*

Christ with Sacred Story Prayer, Sacred Story Rosary is a dynamic prayer discipline for entering further into the key mysteries—the *Sacred Story*—of the entire cosmos. My prayer is that you can find some of the same graces that I have found in praying *Sacred Story Rosary*.

The Father's Love Story approaches the final victory to undo a fateful choice that our first parents, seduced by darkness, unleashed in global history. In the Father's Love Story for the world, the Church will be at the very center of this ongoing drama just as Christ foretold.[7] The triumph is assured so we must take heart, joyfully centering our lives on Christ and his promise to remain with the Church till the end of the age. "Be not afraid!" Mary conceived without sin, pray for us!

Fr. Bill Watson, S.J.
April 12, 2015
Feast of Divine Mercy

FOREWORD COMMENTARY

Most of us, I suspect, have heard of the *Spiritual Exercises* of St. Ignatius. Few of us, and I count myself among the ignorant, despite graduating from a Jesuit university, have any idea what the *Exercises* consist of or demand of the individual who embraces them. In the autumn of 2014 I helped offer a retreat for members of the Order of Malta, and we reflected on a book that attributed Pope Francis' leadership style to his intense dedication to the *Exercises*. To my great annoyance, the author never explained the substance of the *Exercises*.

What a pleasure, then, to encounter Fr. William Watson's *Sacred Story Rosary,* which not only provides a concise description of the *Exercises*, but leads the reader, step-by-step through an application of the *Exercises* to the eternal truths of the Rosary.

When I entered the Dominican Order, nearly half a century ago, we received a Rosary as part of our religious habit, and we gathered each day in the chapel to recite its prayers. Not much has changed in those fifty years; we still gather to share the prayer we Dominicans are so proud of. Some days it offers immense consolation, on others it is simply a task to be "gotten through." Every now and then, though, God rewards us with a moment of insight. A few years ago I discovered that emphasizing one or two words made the prayers a great deal more meaningful.

And then, along comes Fr. Watson's book! It is more than simply the latest reflection on the Mysteries of the Rosary; it is an invitation to enter into the Mysteries in a new way. The genius of St. Ignatius' *Exercises* is the part they play in the larger scheme of one's spiritual life, something an individual traditionally comes to understand under the guidance of a spiritual director.

This is the role Fr. Watson embraces, introducing us to each of the Mysteries of the Rosary, and helping us to see how Christ and His mother are acting in our lives.

When he considers Jesus' passion and death, Fr. Watson asks us to "ponder what God has accomplished in Christ Jesus on my behalf in light of this particular mystery," and observes:

> *Original Sin unleashed upon the world an evolution of rage in the overwhelming grief of divorcing one's self from the ecstasy of intimacy with God and each other. This is Satan's rage which by choice we have made our own. In this rage, human relationships are violated at every level, making sin's greatest trauma that of abandonment and loneliness...In freely absorbing our sins in His Sacred Heart, He is cut-off from experiencing the Father's love, and from those depths forgives us, mending permanently the communion of love that was our birthright with the Trinity and each other.*

I dare say few of us have been asked to meditate quite so deeply or personally on the price of our Redemption! But Fr. Watson doesn't stop there. Exercise ought to make us stronger, so our director asks us to commit to writing what we have learned, transforming a prayer journey for our own unique *Sacred Story*.

One of our Dominican mottos is *contemplare aliis tradere* – to share with others the fruits of our contemplation. If we surrender to Fr. Watson's discipline, we will not come away from this book unchanged. Even if we are too modest ever to refer directly to one of our reflections after reading this book, the exercise itself will give us a great deal to share with others.

Fr. Reginald Martin, OP
Director: The Rosary Center

As with all authentic Christian 'devotions,' the Rosary is so simple that the wider transformative and revolutionary dimensions of its embrace may be missed; neither perceived nor experienced - rather like the disarming simplicity of an uncomplicated, simple, crisp and neat physical formula (e.g. $E = mc2$).

Reading through Bill Watson's *Sacred Story Rosary* reminded me of an incident, many years ago now, whilst accompanying a wonderful man, a Baptist Minister, now deceased, through the Spiritual Exercises of St. Ignatius Loyola. He was someone who could use his imagination to great advantage, and was sharing his experience of the Nativity of Jesus (the 3rd of the Joyful Mysteries of the Rosary).

In his contemplation he was very busy, outside the place where the birth had taken place, cutting wood for Joseph to feed the fire inside. Every so often he would pause his chopping, open the door and push some of his cut wood inside, giving a brief glace at the scene inside. This happened several times.

Then, on this particular occasion, having pushed in yet more chopped wood, as he glanced in, Mary looked up and caught his eye, and said to him, "For goodness sake, if you are coming in, come in! If you are staying out, then stay out!" These sharp, very unexpected, brief words from Mary proved to be deeply transforming and revolutionary for the stunned Baptist Minister. He remained an energetic Baptist Minister and also a leader in popularizing the Ignatian Exercises.

I do believe that Bill Watson has managed to provide in this book an instrument that can facilitate in others their own transforming and revolutionary spiritual experiences. In few words he manages to retain the simplicity of the Mysteries of the Rosary combined with the directness of the Sacred Scripture.

In an admirable and creative manner Bill Watson integrates into the praying of the Rosary the Ignatian suggestions for praying the Scriptures, especially the Gospels (the Preludes and the Points).

The Preludes effectively invite the one praying to do three things. The first is to contextualise the Scripture passage – in large, what is the passage about. The second is to look at my own present context, in relation to the context of the Scripture. The third is to become aware of the desire(s) that arise in me as I become aware of these two contexts and of the relationships opening up between the two contexts; and then to express that desire in the intimacy of prayer.

The Points suggest that I look more closely at the relevant passage of the Scripture, keeping in mind at least the following three dimensions: Who are the Persons in the passage; What are the persons doing in the passage; and, What are the persons saying in the passage; and then to fruitfully be drawn into the intimacy of prayer as a result.

This Bill Watson skillfully and unobtrusively manages and achieves. *Sacred Story Rosary* is clearly the outpouring of Bill Watson's own personal prayer, but this personal experience is imaginatively and creatively reordered so that others, with their own similar, but different life experiences, can enter into their own transformative and revolutionary experience in meeting God through the Scriptural Mysteries of the Rosary of that extraordinary woman, Mary, the Mother of the Lord.

David Keith Townsend, S.J.
Seven Fountains Jesuit Spirituality Centre, Chiang Mai, Thailand

An Ignatian Method of Praying the Rosary

Fidelity to a spiritual discipline requires more than sheer willpower. Many people have begun a new spiritual regimen with dedication but in time the passion wanes. This has happened to me countless times. I knew the Rosary was important when I started praying it but sometimes became bored or distracted when I prayed. Many times I took heart in the comment attributed to St. Therese of Lisieux that she oftentimes fell asleep before she finished the Rosary. She had a child's joy however, because she said the Blessed Mother would finish it for her!

Others could never fall asleep praying the Rosary. After my "Marian awakening," I became friends with Fr. Richard McSorley, S.J. He was known as the "Peace Priest," for his "career" protesting against war.[8] He lived at Georgetown University, as did I, and was deeply devoted to the Blessed Mother and the daily Rosary. There was something both holy and humorous in the way Fr. McSorley prayed the Rosary. He was totally serious in his praying but could rattle off an entire

Rosary in less than 8 minutes. He always wanted to pray a Rosary when we drove places and we could oftentimes get in two or more, even on short trips. If I fell asleep with my own praying of the Rosary, Fr. McSorley would get speeding tickets from Heaven for praying his. He prayed so fast I could not understand the words to the *Paters* and *Aves.*

I mention these two examples as I believe they capture many people's experience of this great prayer. Some get bored or distracted in praying and others rattle off the Mysteries to "get through them" before boredom can set in. Both are better than no Rosary at all. Yet, if I was going to draw some fruit from this most popular of devotional prayers, I needed to find a way to make it my own. I was searching for something more contemplative and spiritually nourishing. The Rosary's Mysteries should engage my heart and my mind without compelling me to race through them (or make me fall asleep).

Twenty years of praying aided by hefty doses of graced inspiration have led me to a profoundly fruitful practice of this great prayer. Here are some insights that have made the Rosary my greatest experience of transcendent prayer.

A "Place to Visit" Rather than just "Rush Past"

Some believe they must focus on the words of the prayers to truly pray the Rosary. Instead, I believe contemplating the Mysteries is the reason for the Rosary. I had to learn—perhaps "give myself permission" is more accurate—not to focus consciously on the "prayers" of the Rosary, but its Mysteries. Another way to say it might be this: the Mysteries are a place to visit, so the prayers are not something to just "get through." Consider this:

I remember learning to drive a stick shift. It was a profound challenge for a kid who was used to automatics. It seemed I would never master the brake/clutch/gas/shift rhythm. When I was learning the stick, the mental attention required for the coordination of all the different steps in the process was extraordinary. With the extra complication of traffic—maybe stopped on a hill with a car practically kissing my back bumper—and it was enough to make me break into a cold sweat.

But one day I realized I was driving while talking to my passengers, tuning the radio, and drinking coffee—without even thinking about the brake, clutch, gas pedal or stick shift! How did that happen? I had learned to drive a stick and no longer needed to consciously pay attention to the details of the process. My brain was still managing all those steps but my mastery of the mechanics had freed me to actually drive. I was going somewhere with people and not thinking about how I was doing it. In other words, the purpose of driving "somewhere" and the enjoyment of doing that, oftentimes with friends, had taken center stage.

This is how I have come to think of the "prayers of the beads" in relation to its Mysteries. Once you have mastered the prayers and their mechanics, you are free to contemplate and pray the Mysteries. You are still praying the *Paters, Aves* and *Glories*, but now they are carrying you as your heart and mind focuses on the most important Mysteries of the universe. The time it takes to cover the prayers is the space of time God gives you for this spiritual contemplation.

Over the last few years, I have noticed something *mysterious* about the space of time it takes me to complete a Rosary. My Rosaries are usually prayed on my evening walks. Some days, I can walk for twenty minutes and others for an hour. For reasons that are not clear to me, the length of time it takes to pray a whole Rosary matches the number of minutes I walk. On twenty minute walk days, the Rosary takes that long to pray, and an hour on sixty minute walk days.

I do not know why this happens, as I am not consciously planning it. What I decided is that the length of time it takes to cover the *Paters, Aves and Glories* expands and contracts precisely because the contemplation of the Mysteries has become my principal reason for praying the Rosary. I want to spend time on those Mysteries and so my walk adjusts to make that happen. Thank you, Lord, for this *mysterious* time of grace.

Ignatian Contemplation of the Mysteries

St. Ignatius used his entire imagination when he reflected on the mysteries of the Lord's life. A typical instruction from his *Spiritual Exercises* on how to "visit" a Gospel scene is that of the Nativity of the Lord.[9] Ignatius wants you to grasp the purpose of what is taking place and to see all the players and practically touch their surroundings—the stage setting for the drama with its time of day, sights, sounds and scents—as you visit the mystery. And he wants you to ask for gifts as you do so because there are specific graces God wants to give you each time pray. So too for the Rosary. God wants you to ask for gifts each time you "visit" the still point of those Mysteries that are relevant for all people and for all time. You can visit the same Mystery hundreds or thousands of times across the arc of your life and it will be new and fresh each time. The Mysteries and the eternal truths they contain are boundless. Each time you visit them, you are at a new point in your own *Sacred Story*. As St. Augustine defined God so too we can define the Rosary's Mysteries: "Beauty, ever ancient, ever new." [10]

A Five-fold Contemplation

Influenced by so many years with the *Spiritual Exercises* and the *Examen* prayer (the *Spiritual Exercises* in miniature), I developed an Ignatian method for visiting these universal Mysteries of the cosmos each time I pray the Rosary. There are five "movements" in my contemplation of each Mystery. Here they are in brief:

✳ First, I allow myself to become conscious of the Mystery's truth—I announce it to myself and let it become present.

✳ Second, I reflect on what God has accomplished in Christ Jesus or Mary on my behalf in light of this particular mystery. I want to understand *how* what God has accomplished in Christ and/or Mary is a model for me and a high ideal which I am being invited to model in my own life.

✳ Third, I pray to understand how this universal Mystery uniquely applies to my own *Sacred Story*: what is my greatest inspiration to live its ideal in my life and how does God uniquely invite me to fulfill the truth of this Mystery?

✳ Fourth, I examine my own life in light of how I have not lived up to the ideal that I am invited to by this Mystery. This is my time to ask for mercy and forgiveness in light of wasted opportunities. I want to know the suffering caused to me and others for being less than diligent in fulfilling God's plan *for me* in light of this particular Mystery.

✳ Fifth, I close with a prayer of thanksgiving to Christ and Mary for walking the path of the Mystery in complete fidelity to the Father's will. I pray that I can be inspired by the Mystery's high ideal once again and that I too, can more faithfully live it in my own *Sacred Story*.

In this five-fold method of praying each Mystery, we have: a summary of the Mystery's universal implications for salvation history; a contemplation on what that Mystery entails; a reflection on how the Mystery might apply to us personally; an examination of conscience that allows us to measure your *Sacred Story* to the Mystery's ideal; and a closing prayer of gratitude. Praying each Mystery in this progressive way models the classic structure of the Ignatian *Examen.*[11]

How to Make Sacred Story Rosary Your Own

You are invited to reflect on each of the Mysteries of the Sacred Story Rosary. Ask the Holy Spirit to understand the "heart" of each Mystery so that you can feel in your soul and know its gift. See what it means for the whole human race. Then, using the suggested personal application, see how the Mystery is elemental to your own *Sacred Story*. Discern the general and particular ways you are tempted to evade its call or fall short of its ideal. Then make the closing prayer your own so that it is heartfelt and responds to where you are in your life each time you pray it.

When I pray the Rosary this way, I don't mechanically tick off each of these five movements in order. Let me remind you about my example of learning to drive a stick shift. I *know* the five themes as they have become part of my heart. I contemplate them as the Spirit moves me in the time God gives me to move through the bead's prayers.

Some days I am awed by the truth of the Mystery and spend most of my time considering what Mary and/or Jesus accomplished for me and the world. Other days I will spend the bulk of my time examining my life alongside the Mystery's ideal. Other days I move all over the place with the five themes. Still other days I may be totally preoccupied by a triumph or a tragedy. Not to worry! Like the Psalms, there is something in each Mystery that will be relevant to at that time.

God is really in charge when you pray the Rosary and you will "visit" what you need to visit and it will be new each day. It is good to ask the Holy Spirit *for the grace* to focus your heart on what is most elemental for you at the point in your day or life that you are praying the Mystery. The important thing is this: I know the five themes "by heart" in the same way that I know the *Aves, Paters, and Glories* by heart.

So that you too can learn these themes by heart, this book concludes with your own chapter called, "My Sacred Story Rosary." There is a template for all the Mysteries meant to be filled in with your short version of each of the five themes.

After you have learned the Mysteries of Sacred Story Rosary "by heart," I invite you to concisely summarize each of the twenty mystery's five reflections in your own words. This way when you pray the Rosary in the future, you will have a way to pray and reflect the most fundamental truths of the cosmos in light of your own unique *Sacred* Story and the significance of our own time in the course salvation history; both for the Church the world. It is a homework assignment, but remember that all prayer involves labor. That is why St. Ignatius called his masterwork *The Spiritual Exercises!*

How to Pray the Rosary

The Rosary is one of the most popular ways to pray and reflect on the lives of Jesus and Mary. It is one of the most widely practiced devotions in the history of the Catholic Church. In praying the rosary, remember that it is less something to "get through" than it is a "place to visit."

1. With the crucifix, make the Sign of the Cross and pray the Apostles' Creed:

I believe in God, the Father Almighty, Creator of Heaven and earth; and in Jesus Christ, His only Son Our Lord, Who was conceived by the Holy Spirit, born of the Virgin Mary, suffered under Pontius Pilate, was crucified, died, and was buried. He descended into Hell; the third day He rose again from the dead; He ascended into Heaven, and sits at the right hand of God, the Father almighty; from thence He shall come to judge the living and the dead.

I believe in the Holy Spirit, the holy Catholic Church, the communion of saints, the forgiveness of sins, the resurrection of the body and life everlasting. Amen.

2. With the first bead beyond the crucifix, pray the *Our Father:*

Our Father, Who art in heaven,
Hallowed be Thy Name. Thy Kingdom come.
Thy Will be done, on earth as it is in Heaven.
Give us this day our daily bread.
And forgive us our trespasses,
As we forgive those who trespass against us.
And lead us not into temptation,
But deliver us from evil. Amen!

3. With the next three beads, pray the *Hail Mary* on each; one for faith, one for hope, one for charity.

Hail Mary, Full of Grace, The Lord is with thee.
Blessed art thou among women, and blessed is the fruit
of thy womb, Jesus. Holy Mary, Mother of God,
pray for us sinners now, and at the hour of death.
Amen!

4. After the three *Hail Marys*, pray the *Glory Be:*

Glory be to the Father, and to the Son,
and to the Holy Spirit.
As it was in the beginning, is now, and ever shall be,
World without end. Amen!

5. (Repeat 6 through 10 for each of the five Mysteries in the

four different sets: *Joy, Sorrow, Glory* and *Light*. A single Mystery includes one bead for the *Our Father*, ten beads for the ten *Hail Marys*, and a closing *Glory Be*).

6. On the last of the beads *before* the three-way joint (usually a holy medal), announce the first mystery and pray the *Our Father*.

7. Beginning with the first bead on the left beyond the three-way joint, pray ten *Hail Marys*, one for each bead. After the last *Hail Mary*, always close with the *Glory Be*.

8. After the *Glory Be*, many Catholics pray the prayer taught to the children of Fatima by the angel:

"Oh my Jesus, forgive us our sins, save us from the fires of hell and bring all souls to heaven, especially those most in need of your mercy."

Others use the Jesus Prayer after the *Glory Be*:

"Lord Jesus Christ, Son of the Living God, have mercy on me a sinner."

9. Proceed to the next Mystery and repeat the process, focusing your heart on the meditations of the Blessed Mother and the Lord's lives that the Mystery encompasses.

10. After the conclusion of the fifth mystery, pray the *Hail Holy Queen.*

Hail, holy Queen, Mother of mercy, our life, our sweetness and our hope. To thee do we cry, poor banished children of Eve. To thee to we send up our sighs, mourning and weeping in this valley of tears. Turn, then, most gracious advocate, thine eyes of mercy toward us, and after this, our exile, show unto us the blessed fruit of thy womb, Jesus. O clement, O loving, O sweet Virgin Mary.
V. Pray for us, O holy Mother of God.
R. That we may be made worthy of the promises of Christ.

9. Concluding Prayer (optional):

O God whose only begotten Son, by his life, death, and resurrection has purchased for us the rewards of eternal salvation, grant, we beseech thee, that by meditating upon the mysteries of the most Holy Rosary of the Blessed Virgin Mary, we may imitate what they contain and obtain what they promise, through the same Christ, Our Lord. Amen.

Close with the Sign of the Cross, using the crucifix of the rosary. Many offer one *Our Father,* one *Hail Mary,* and one *Glory Be* at the conclusion of each rosary for the needs and intentions of the Holy Father.

The Mysteries of Joy

The Annunciation to Mary

The Visitation of Mary

The Nativity of the Lord

The Presentation of the Child Jesus in the Temple

The Finding of Our Lord in the Temple

These Mysteries are generally prayed on

Monday & Thursday

The Annunciation to Mary

In the sixth month, the angel Gabriel was sent from God to a town of Galilee called Nazareth, to a virgin betrothed to a man named Joseph, of the house of David, and the virgin's name was Mary. And coming to her, he said, "Hail, favored one! The Lord is with you." But she was greatly troubled at what was said and pondered what sort of greeting this might be. Then the angel said to her, "Do not be afraid, Mary, for you have found favor with God. And Behold, you will conceive in your womb and bear a son, and you shall name him Jesus. He will be great and will be called Son of the Most High, and the Lord God will give him the throne of David his father, and he will rule over the house of Jacob forever, and of his kingdom there will be no end." But Mary said to the angel, "How can this be, since I have no relations with a man?" And the angel said to her in reply, "The holy Spirit will come upon you, and the power of the Most High will overshadow you. Therefore the child to be born will be called holy, the Son of God. And behold, Elizabeth, your relative, has also conceived a son in her old age, and this is the sixth month for her who was called barren; for nothing will be impossible for God." Mary said, "Behold, I am the handmaid of the Lord. May it be done to me according to your word." Then the angel departed from her. *(Lk 1: 26-38)*

THE HEART OF THE MYSTERY

✳*I speak the mystery in my heart allowing its truth to shape my time of prayer.*

Mary said "Yes" to God with all her heart, mind and strength, the first of Abraham's descendants to do so, although at first she doubted and was fearful.

✳ *I now ponder what God has accomplished in Christ Jesus and Mary on my behalf in light of this particular mystery:*

Mary's "Yes" to the conception, birth, life, death and resurrection of the Father's Son set in motion God's plan to redeem the human race *by and through human cooperation.*" She was the first of our race to respond fully to God in her life's mission. We know from her example that we are never to surrender to fear, but to always trust the Lord when he calls us to follow Him. Though unable to understand how the promise He places in our hearts can be fulfilled, we see through Mary's eyes that "nothing will be impossible for God" (Lk 1:37).

✳ *I now pray to understand how the truth of this universal*

Mystery uniquely applies to my own Sacred Story:

What is the deepest hope I have for my life? What grace of surrender do I seek to say "Yes" to God with all my heart, mind and strength? What fears and doubts do I have that I need to hear God say to me: "Do not be afraid, for nothing will be impossible for God.

✳ *I now examine my own life in light of how I have or have not lived up to the ideal to which the Mystery invites me to model:*

Where have I said "Yes" to the work God wants to accomplish in me? What are the specific fears that keep me from following the call of Christ in my heart? Do I avoid silence so as to block the voice of God in my heart? What are my doubts about God's fidelity that bring me confusion and despair? Do I surrender to pessimism in thinking it is too late for God to accomplish in me a work that will bear fruit unto eternity?

✳ *I close with a prayer of thanksgiving to Christ and Mary for walking the path of the Mystery in complete fidelity to the Father's will. I pray that I can be inspired by the Mystery's high ideal once again and that I too, can more faithfully live it in my own Sacred Story.*

Mary, thank you for your complete "Yes" to the Father's will. Please pray for me to have the grace and patience to overcome my fears of saying "Yes" to His plan for my own Sacred Story. May I never doubt God's power to overcome all obstacles in fulfilling His will in my life. May I always turn to you for your intercession when I am afraid or doubting, as I know you will hear my prayers. Amen!

THE VISITATION OF MARY

During those days Mary set out and traveled to the hill country in haste to a town of Judah, where she entered the house of Zechariah and greeted Elizabeth. When Elizabeth heard Mary's greeting, the infant leaped in her womb, and Elizabeth, filled with the holy Spirit, cried out in a loud voice and said, "Most blessed are you among women, and blessed is the fruit of your womb. And how does this happen to me, that the mother of my Lord should come to me? For at the moment the sound of your greeting reached my ears, the infant in my womb leaped for joy. Blessed are you who believed that what was spoken to you by the Lord would be fulfilled."

And Mary said: "My soul proclaims the greatness of the Lord; my spirit rejoices in God my savior. For he has looked upon his handmaid's lowliness; behold, from now on will all ages call me blessed." *(Lk 13:9-48)*

THE HEART OF THE MYSTERY

✴ I speak the mystery in my heart allowing its truth to shape my time of prayer:

Blessed Mary, you reveal in the Visitation that authentic love always leads me out of myself towards communion with and sacrifice for others.

✴ I now ponder what God has accomplished in Christ Jesus and Mary on my behalf in light of this particular mystery:

Mary's Visitation to Elizabeth shows that true holiness is a gift that must lead beyond one's self. For the gift of God's love is always apostolic, calling me to witness to others the blessing, love and mercy God has lavished on me. Mary's Visitation demonstrates how God searches for those in need, no matter the danger the mission presents. Mary's Visitation gives evidence that works of charity, however humble, produce fruit that endures to eternity.

✴ I now pray to understand how the truth of this universal Mystery uniquely applies to my own Sacred Story:

What is my deepest hope to extend myself in loving communion and sacrifice for others?" How do the gifts of faith and mercy God has shown to me need sharing with those closest to me, especially my family? What missions of charity does God invite me to undertake, to bring hope and consolation to those in need? Who on the edge of my society does the Lord invite me to visit with comfort and friendship?

✳ *I now examine my own life in light of how I have or have not lived up to the ideal to which the Mystery invites me to model:*

How do I resist extending myself in loving service to my family and friends? Who close to me do I refuse to care for because it would inconvenience me? What type of self-centeredness is my greatest weakness? What person or group do I dismiss as undeserving of my charity or care? What is the main fear or stumbling block that keeps me from fuller communion with and sacrifice for others?

✳ *I close with a prayer of thanksgiving to Christ and Mary for walking the path of the Mystery in complete fidelity to the Father's will. I pray that I can be inspired by the Mystery's high ideal once again and that I too, can more faithfully live it in my own Sacred Story.*

Mary, I thank you for your model of charity and self-forgetfulness. Please intercede for me to your Son for the patience and mercy I need in my struggle to follow your example of selfless love in my own Sacred Story." Amen!

THE NATIVITY OF THE LORD

While they were there, the time came for her to have her child, and she gave birth to her firstborn son. She wrapped him in swaddling clothes and laid him in a manger, because there was no room for them in the inn. Now there were shepherds in that region living in the fields and keeping the night watch over their flock. The angel of the Lord appeared to them and the glory of the Lord shone around them, and they were struck with great fear. The angel said to them, "Do not be afraid; for behold, I proclaim to you good news of great joy that will be for all the people. For today in the city of David a savior has been born for you who is Messiah and Lord. And this will be a sign for you: you will find an infant wrapped in swaddling clothes and lying in a manger." And suddenly there was a multitude of the heavenly host with the angel, praising God and saying: "Glory to God in the highest and on earth peace to those on whom his favor rests." *(Lk 2: 6-14)*

THE HEART OF THE MYSTERY

✳ *I speak the mystery in my heart allowing its truth to shape my time of prayer.*

Mary and Joseph, the Nativity of Christ reveals that family is the greatest gift God grants to those made in the Divine image and likeness; an icon of the Trinity's Love and the cradle from which God redeemed the human race.

✳ *I now ponder what God has accomplished in Christ Jesus and Mary on my behalf in light of this particular mystery:*

Overcoming fear and doubt, Mary and Joseph triumph by God's power and grace to bring the human race our Eternal Redeemer. Human nature, through whose free choice brought death to our race, is granted by God the inestimable gift of helping rectify sin's shame. God in Jesus invites human cooperation in humankind's redemption. The Nativity is the hope for all those called to marriage and having children that God provides all necessary grace to participate in Christ's salvific mission of nuptial union. The lowly place of Christ's birth reveals that a wealth of love, not the riches of the world, is the sustenance a child needs to thrive. The Nativity is the Father's icon that every human child from the moment of conception till natural death is a cherished son or daughter of the Father and blessed with a unique vocation for Christ's redemptive work.

✳ *I now pray to understand how the truth of this universal Mystery uniquely applies to my own Sacred Story:*

How does the Holy Family reveal my most profound hope for family love? What salvific work can I accomplish with Christ by my fidelity to my own family or marriage? What is my desire for motherhood or fatherhood in bringing forth new life according to God's plan? How does God call me to greater trust and hope to surrender in love to my family? Do I understand that a deep faith and not the riches of the world is the true foundation of marriage and family life? Do I see my own life as blessed by Father with a singular mission in the work of Redemption?

✳ *I now examine my own life in light of how I have or have not lived up to the ideal to which the Mystery invites me to model:*

Where have I opened myself to "holy family life" by allowing God's plan to come to term in my story? What is the main fear or stumbling block that keeps me at a distance from sharing fully in my family life and/or the fruitfulness of motherhood or fatherhood? Do I allow excessive concern for wealth to deter me from generosity in choices for my family?

✳ *I close with a prayer of thanksgiving to Christ and Mary for walking the path of the Mystery in complete fidelity to the Father's will. I pray that I can be inspired by the Mystery's high ideal once again and that I too, can more faithfully live it in my own Sacred Story.*

Mary and Joseph, thank you for overcoming all your fears and doubts so that Christ the Lord could be born in your Holy Family as our Savior and Redeemer. Help me achieve holiness of family life. Please intercede so that obstacles of fear and mistrust may not prevent me from   accepting my full vocation or doubting that God has chosen me for a unique mission in Christ's salvific work. Please protect all parents and children and bless the Church's mission of proclaiming the beauty of marital love according to God's plan. Amen!

The Presentation of the Child Jesus
In the Temple

When the days were completed for their purification according to the law of Moses, they took him up to Jerusalem to present him to the Lord, just as it is written in the law of the Lord, "Every male that opens the womb shall be consecrated to the Lord," and to offer the sacrifice of "a pair of turtledoves or two young pigeons," in accordance with the dictate in the law of the Lord. Now there was a man in Jerusalem whose name was Simeon. This man was righteous and devout, awaiting the consolation of Israel, and the holy Spirit was upon him. It had been revealed to him by the holy Spirit that he should not see death before he had seen the Messiah of the Lord. He came in the Spirit into the temple; and when the parents brought in the child Jesus to perform the custom of the law in regard to him, he took him into his arms and blessed God, saying: "Now, Master, you may let your servant go in peace, according to your word, for my eyes have seen your salvation, which you prepared in sight of all the peoples, a light for revelation to the Gentiles, and glory for your people Israel." The child's father and mother were amazed at what was said about him; and Simeon blessed them and said to Mary his mother, "Behold, this child is destined for the fall and rise of many in Israel, and to be a sign that will be contradicted (and you yourself a sword will pierce) so that the thoughts of many hearts may be revealed." *(Lk 2:22-35)*

THE HEART OF THE MYSTERY

 I speak the mystery in my heart allowing its truth to shape my time of prayer.

Mary and Joseph, you demonstrate how to achieve holiness by placing God first with docile and obedient hearts, fulfilling the gift of His holy law in all your thoughts, words and deeds.

 I now ponder what God has accomplished in Christ Jesus and Mary on my behalf in light of this particular mystery:

The most exalted mother and father in human history model that no parents are above God's holy laws. God honors Joseph and Mary in the Presentation of the Child Jesus by Simeon's prophecy, revealing the momentous role each is to play in Christ's salvation of the human race. In their humble submission to the Law of Moses they disclose the pattern of sanctification for all married people. All parents who submit in humble obedience to the laws of Christ in the Church will likewise be honored by Christ, with a blessed marriage that bears fruit for the eternal Kingdom of the Father.

✳ *I now pray to understand how the truth of this universal Mystery uniquely applies to my own Sacred Story:*

"What is my deepest desire to model the humble obedience of the Holy Family by submitting to the holy laws of God in my own life—in my thoughts, my words and my deeds? As a parent, how can I understand the doctrines of Christ proclaimed by the Church as a holy path to peace and fulfillment and not a restriction of my personal freedoms? *"How I love your law, Lord! I study it all day long (Ps 119: 97)."* How does the model of Mary and Joseph's full participation in the rituals of the Covenant inform the sacramental life of the Church that I am invited to engage for myself and my family?

✳ *I now examine my own life in light of how I have or have not lived up to the ideal to which the Mystery invites me to model:*

When have I been consoled by humbly and obediently surrendering to God's holy laws? What doctrines of Christ as taught by the Church do I find myself resisting regularly? Do I openly challenge them by my actions in my life or with my family? How faithful am I in living a full sacramental life in the Church for myself and for my family? What healing and graces does God desire to give me so that I might more faithfully follow Christ in His Church?

✳ *I close with a prayer of thanksgiving to Christ and Mary for walking the path of the Mystery in complete fidelity to the Father's will. I pray that I can be inspired by the Mystery's high ideal once again and that I too, can more faithfully live it in my own Sacred Story.*

Mary and Joseph, your model of humility and obedience reveals the power of God who promises to raise the lowly and confound the arrogant. You give consolation to all married people by showing them the path of lasting peace, joy and glory. Help all parents lead their families to the lasting fulfillment the laws of Christ invite. Intercede for me too for the humility and obedience to fulfill God's holy law, so that my Sacred Story will be blessed and contribute to the glorious work of the Kingdom of Christ.

The Finding of Our Lord in the Temple

Each year his parents went to Jerusalem for the feast of Passover, and when he was twelve years old, they went up according to festival custom. After they had completed its days, as they were returning, the boy Jesus remained behind in Jerusalem, but his parents did not know it. Thinking that he was in the caravan, they journeyed for a day and looked for him among their relatives and acquaintances, but not finding him, they returned to Jerusalem to look for him. After three days they found him in the temple, sitting in the midst of the teachers, listening to them and asking them questions, and all who heard him were astounded at his understanding and his answers. When his parents saw him, they were astonished, and his mother said to him, "Son, why have you done this to us? Your father and I have been looking for you with great anxiety." And he said to them, "Why were you looking for me? Did you not know that I must be in my Father's house?" But they did not understand what he said to them. He went down with them and came to Nazareth, and was obedient to them; and his mother kept all these things in her heart. And Jesus advanced [in] wisdom and age and favor before God and man. *(Lk 2: 41-52)*

THE HEART OF THE MYSTERY

 I speak the mystery in my heart allowing its truth to shape my time of prayer.

Lord Jesus, you manifest in the Temple that every child is a unique being created in the Divine image whose parents are to cherish and surrender back to God so as to accept their incomparable mission in life.

 I now ponder what God has accomplished in Christ Jesus and Mary on my behalf in light of this particular mystery:

Mary and Joseph fully embraced the joy and anxiety of childrearing. As Jesus grew to adulthood, Mary and Joseph accepted even that which they did not understand as the path the Father had chosen for His Christ. Mary and Joseph show all parents that children are to be loved, disciplined and formed in the ways of Faith, but surrendered to God so they are free to claim their unique mission in life. Jesus shows all children that they must listen to God's voice above all others and responsibly embrace the Kingdom mission God has placed in their heart from the very beginning. In this Mystery, Mary and Joseph model the highest expression of parental sacrificial love for a child as a unique person and a gift from God.

✳ *I now pray to understand how the truth of this universal Mystery uniquely applies to my own Sacred Story:*

What is my deepest desire as a parent to allow my children to grow to their fullness in God's image and likeness? What is my desire as a son or daughter for the support of parents who will lovingly discipline and guide me so I can realize my life's promise in God's image and likeness? What is my hope as a parent, son or daughter to bear the anxiety that responsible autonomy requires for my family to imitate the Holy Family?

✳ *I now examine my own life in light of how I have or have not lived up to the ideal to which the Mystery invites me to model:*

Do I as a parent strive to live the highest ideal of parental love as modeled by Mary and Joseph? Where do I fall short by being too controlling or lax in my love for them? Do I as a child take responsibility in allowing myself to be led to the fullness of life in God's image and likeness, even when it conflicts with my parents' wishes or plans? Do I, as a child or parent, pray for the grace to forgive the other in the face of love's failings and imperfections?

✳ *I close with a prayer of thanksgiving to Christ and Mary for walking the path of the Mystery in complete fidelity to the Father's will. I pray that I can be inspired by the Mystery's high ideal once again and that I too, can more faithfully live it in my own Sacred Story.*

Mary and Joseph, your joys and your sorrows in raising Christ Jesus so he could follow the Father's will, were like no other in human history. Pray that I may receive the grace, as a parent, son or daughter, to desire love's highest expression in relation to my children or my own parents. Pray that I may receive the grace so my Sacred Story models God's image and likeness so that my Kingdom Mission may come to fruition. Amen!

THE MYSTERIES OF SORROW

THE AGONY IN THE GARDEN

THE SCOURGING AT THE PILLAR

THE CROWNING WITH THORNS

THE CARRYING OF THE CROSS

THE CRUCIFIXION AND DEATH OF THE LORD

These Mysteries are generally prayed on

Tuesday & Friday

THE AGONY IN THE GARDEN

Then going out he went, as was his custom, to the Mount of Olives, and the disciples followed him. When he arrived at the place he said to them, "Pray that you may not undergo the test." After withdrawing about a stone's throw from them and kneeling, he prayed, saying, "Father, if you are willing, take this cup away from me; still, not my will but yours be done." And to strengthen him an angel from heaven appeared to him. He was in such agony and he prayed so fervently that his sweat became like drops of blood falling on the ground. When he rose from prayer and returned to his disciples, he found them sleeping from grief. He said to them, "Why are you sleeping? Get up and pray that you may not undergo the test." *(Lk 22:39-45)*

"And this is the verdict, that the light came into the world, but people preferred darkness to light, because their works were evil." *(Jn 3:19)*

THE HEART OF THE MYSTERY

✳ *I speak the mystery in my heart allowing its truth to shape my time of prayer.*

Christ Jesus, the Son of Man, suffered the full measure of humankind's spiritual, psychological and physical terror loosed in all history by our sin in turning away from the love of the Father.

✳ *I now ponder what God has accomplished in Christ Jesus on my behalf in light of this particular mystery:*

In His agony, Jesus deconstructs the towers of Babel that humankind has created, and faces the darkness, power, anger, violence, self-aggrandizement, arrogance, lust and greed that slander the Father's way of smallness, forgiveness and surrender. In his agony, He faces what is most shameful, dark, twisted, anti-human and violent in our hearts. He freely carries in His Sacred Heart the human evil of love betrayed and its dark consequences for all people and for all time.

✳ *I now pray to understand how the truth of this universal Mystery uniquely applies to my own Sacred Story:*

What is my deepest desire as a follower of Jesus to confront the towers of Babel that human arrogance and evil have constructed in my family, relationships and society? What is my noblest aspiration to suffer with Christ the spiritual, psychological and physical dread of marginalization that will result in being counted as one of His followers?

✴ *I now examine my own life in light of how I have or have not lived up to the ideal to which the Mystery invites me to model:*

Have I directly confronted any darkness and shame resulting from my or my family's unholy habits, thoughts, words and deeds? Do I "watch and pray" to acknowledge that I share in evil's reign and the marginalization of the righteous who stand with Christ and His Church? Do I face the consequences of what has gone wrong in my life and agree to "stay awake" with Christ suffering in the world today? Do I turn to Christ and allow Him to shoulder my dread and terror when it is too much for me to bear?

✴ *I close with a prayer of thanksgiving to Christ for walking the path of the Mystery in complete fidelity to the Father's will. I pray that I can be inspired by the Mystery's high ideal once again and that I too, can more faithfully live it in my own Sacred Story.*

Lord Jesus, thank you for freely enduring the full consequences of evil's terror and dread in the corruption of human hearts and minds. Thank you for confronting it first at your birth, in the arrogant pride of a despot who slaughtered the innocents, seeking to kill you; at the beginning of your public ministry when Satan tempted you to subvert the Father's plan for salvation by using worldly powers; and now, in Gethsemane, your final "yes" to entering the darkest nightmares of the human mind and heart. May I always stay awake to "watch and pray" with you, so my *Sacred Story* may be forever united with yours. Amen!

THE SCOURGING AT THE PILLAR

The chief priests and the elders persuaded the crowds to ask for Barabbas but to destroy Jesus. The governor said to them in reply, "Which of the two do you want me to release to you?" They answered, "Barabbas!" Pilate said to them, "Then what shall I do with Jesus called Messiah?" They all said, "Let him be crucified!" But he said, "Why? What evil has he done?" They only shouted the louder, "Let him be crucified!" When Pilate saw that he was not succeeding at all, but that a riot was breaking out instead, he took water and washed his hands in the sight of the crowd, saying, "I am innocent of this man's blood. Look to it yourselves." And the whole people said in reply, "His blood be upon us and upon our children." Then he released Barabbas to them, but after he had Jesus scourged, he handed him over to be crucified. *(Mt 27: 20-26)*

THE HEART OF THE MYSTERY

✳ I speak the mystery in my heart allowing its truth to shape my time of prayer.

Christ Jesus, the Son of Man, suffered the full weight of humanity's acts of torture, war and the physical infirmities unleashed in all of human history by every choice, individual and corporate, to turn from the light and the love of the Father.

✳ I now ponder what God has accomplished in Christ Jesus on my behalf in light of this particular mystery:

In His sentencing to death and scourging, Jesus bears the full weight of every innocent person unjustly sentenced and tortured. He bears the pain and physical infirmities of sickness and disease due to original sin in all of humankind. He is the victim who takes our place for the evils of war, genocide and violence unleashed since time immemorial. He the innocent, stands accused on our behalf, and is scourged so that by his wounds we can be healed (Is 53:5; 1 Pt 2:24).

✳ I now pray to understand how the truth of this universal Mystery uniquely applies to my own Sacred Story:

What is my deepest desire to act nobly when unjustly accused? How do I desire to stand in for the weak who are violated and abused by the arrogant? What are my aspirations to bear my share of the responsibility for the violence of war and genocide perpetrated by institutions seeking power over others? How do I wish to honor my mother and father in the infirmity of their old age? How do I want to be remembered for facing courageously the diminishment caused by injury and illness?

✳ *I now examine my own life in light of how I have or have not lived up to the ideal to which the Mystery invites me to model:*

Have I unjustly accused others and led to their suffering? Do I remain silent while the innocent are reproached or harmed? Do I give consent by my silence to institutions or states that place more value in wealth and control than human life? Do I challenge ongoing war as means countries to overcome violence? Do I accept responsibility for any physical suffering or diminishment I have caused myself or others, or do I seek instead to escape the consequences and let others pay the price?

✳ *I close with a prayer of thanksgiving to Christ for walking the path of the Mystery in complete fidelity to the Father's will. I pray that I can be inspired by the Mystery's high ideal once again and that I too, can more faithfully live it in my own Sacred Story.*

Lord Jesus, I am filled with both overwhelming grief and thanksgiving that you, the Innocent One, took my place and suffered the consequences for the wrongs that I have done. Your incomparable love and humility shatters my pride and makes me shed tears of gratitude. Please protect all the innocent and remember in your scourging all of us who suffer the physical burdens and violence of original sin in our bodies. Help me to always suffer injustice with nobility and physical suffering with fortitude so that my *Sacred Story* can be forever joined with your own. Amen!

THE CROWNING WITH THORNS

So Pilate said to him, "Then you are a king?" Jesus answered, "You say I am a king. For this I was born and for this I came into the world, to testify to the truth. Everyone who belongs to the truth listens to my voice." Pilate said to him, "What is truth?" When he had said this, he again went out to the Jews and said to them, "I find no guilt in him. But you have a custom that I release one prisoner to you at Passover. Do you want me to release to you the King of the Jews?" They cried out again, "Not this one but Barabbas!" Now Barabbas was a revolutionary. And the soldiers wove a crown out of thorns and placed it on his head, and clothed him in a purple cloak, and they came to him and said, "Hail, King of the Jews!" And they struck him repeatedly. *(Jn 18: 37-19: 2-3)*

THE HEART OF THE MYSTERY

✳ *I speak the mystery in my heart allowing its truth to shape my time of prayer.*

Christ Jesus, you triumph as King over the father of lies, giving witness to the Truth about God and human nature that evil sought to corrupt by spiritual, moral and intellectual treachery.

✳ *I now ponder what God has accomplished in Christ Jesus on my behalf in light of this particular mystery:*

In His crowning with thorns, Christ Jesus shatters the world of lies and cunning meant to destroy human nature and God's creation. He is King, and "the Way and the Truth, and the Life" (Jn 14: 6; 18: 37-38). Christ bore witness to the Truth and received a crown of thorns as the glory of all those who suffer contempt, mockery, humiliation and all those marginalized, threatened, tortured or killed for witnessing to the truth about God and human nature. Christ Jesus, in his glorious crowning, promises eternal life to all who stand with Him in the Church as witnesses to His Truth in this present age.

✳ *I now pray to understand how the truth of this universal Mystery uniquely applies to my own Sacred Story:*

What is my deepest desire to witness to Christ's truth in the face of evil's reign of moral and intellectual deceit in the present age? What strength do I seek from Christ to endure graciously mockery, cynicism and contempt? What graces do I need from Jesus so that I can stand firm with Him in the Church and humbly defend the truth about God and human nature? What courage do I seek from the King so that I am never ashamed of Him and His words? (Lk 9: 26)

✳ *I now examine my own life in light of how I have or have not lived up to the ideal to which the Mystery invites me to model:*

Do I speak the truth in my thoughts, words and deeds? Do I stand with Christ crucified when culture denies human nature as a creation in the Divine image and likeness? Am I easily pressured to conform to moral and intellectual truths I know to be false and contrary to God's holy law? Do I resist examining my own lifestyle and habits that are morally inconsistent with Christ who is the Way, the Truth and the Life? Am I ashamed of Christ and his words? Do I deny knowing Him by not supporting His bride, the Church, in her mission of speaking truth to the powers of the present age?

✳ *I close with a prayer of thanksgiving to Christ for walking the path of the Mystery in complete fidelity to the Father's will. I pray that I can be inspired by the Mystery's high ideal once again and that I too, can more faithfully live it in my own Sacred Story.*

Dear Lord Jesus, your holy head was pierced by a crown of every sacrilegious lie and insult denying the Truth of God and human nature. Your humility transforms the crown of treachery into a crown of light showing all of us the way to eternal life. Dear Lord Jesus, King of love, truth and humility, allow me to stand fast with you in the Church when she is slapped, mocked and brutally pierced by the falsehoods of this present age. May you give me the grace to stand by your side as a witness to the truth about God and human nature made in the Divine image. May I share in your shaming so I can share your crown of victory in my own *Sacred Story*. Amen!

The Carrying of the Cross

And when they had mocked him, they stripped him of the purple cloak, dressed him in his own clothes, and led him out to crucify him. They pressed into service a passer-by, Simon, a Cyrenian, who was coming in from the country, the father of Alexander and Rufus, to carry his cross. They brought him to the place of Golgotha (which is translated Place of the Skull. *(Mk 15: 20-22)*

THE HEART OF THE MYSTERY

✳ *I speak the mystery in my heart allowing its truth to shape my time of prayer.*

Christ Jesus, the cross you willingly carried was the full burden of suffering, fatigue, hopelessness and drudgery initiated by humankind's rejection of the Father's love"

✳ *I now ponder what God has accomplished in Christ Jesus on my behalf in light of this particular mystery:*

Christ Jesus was willingly crushed under the load of history's sin—our sins—the weight of our perdition we could never carry. He walked to the end every dark tortured path of each person who turned from God, to fully share their shame and humiliation. He faced the full hatred of every jeering crowd who has blasphemed God and God's creation in human nature. Christ Jesus has made the unendurable road of human suffering caused by sin, a highway of grace to the Father.

✳ *I now pray to understand how the truth of this universal Mystery uniquely applies to my own Sacred Story:*

What burden of sin's legacy in my own life does Christ Jesus lovingly carry for me? What selfish rejection of God that creates shame and humiliation does He freely forgive? What daily crosses has Christ asked me to carry in my body, mind or spirit so that I might share in his triumphant glory? What commitment that will demand life-long endurance and patience is Christ lovingly inviting me to walk with Him and with others? What is my hope for accepting that particular cross of sin and darkness that is part of my family legacy that it may end with me?

✳ *I now examine my own life in light of how I have or have not lived up to the ideal to which the Mystery invites me to model:*

Do I let myself acknowledge the sin in my life that Christ Jesus walked to his death to forgive? Do I honor the humiliation and shame he endured by giving him the joy of regularly forgiving my sins? Do I place on others the burden of my own sin and darkness, by making them carry my anger, selfishness and the consequences of my lusts? Am I a bystander when the Church is forced on the road to Calvary in the present age?

✳ *I close with a prayer of thanksgiving to Christ for walking the path of the Mystery in complete fidelity to the Father's will. I pray that I can be inspired by the Mystery's high ideal once again and that I too, can more faithfully live it in my own Sacred Story.*

Dear Lord Jesus, I bend my knee in tearful thanksgiving for carrying my sin and freeing me from the burden of eternal death. My gratitude knows no bounds for your tenderness and docility, as you were condemned on my account. May I never avoid carrying the small crosses for my own and others' sins. May I have the courage to walk with Your Church on her own glorious road to Calvary in each step of my *Sacred Story*. Amen!

The Crucifixion and Death of the Lord

When they came to the place called the Skull, they crucified him and the criminals there, one on his right, the other on his left. Then Jesus said, "Father, forgive them, they know not what they do." They divided his garments by casting lots. It was now about noon and darkness came over the whole land until three in the afternoon because of an eclipse of the sun. Then the veil of the temple was torn down the middle. Jesus cried out in a loud voice, "Father, into your hands I commend my spirit"; and when he had said this he breathed his last. The centurion who witnessed what had happened, glorified God and said, "This man was innocent beyond doubt." *(Lk 23: 33-34; 44-47)*

THE HEART OF THE MYSTERY

✳ *I speak the mystery in my heart allowing its truth to shape my time of prayer.*

Christ Jesus, in your crucifixion and death you bury in your Sacred Heart the abandonment and separation from the Father, sin's most evil curse, and in forgiving us, destroy Satan's reign of death, opening the way to eternal love.

✳ *I now ponder what God has accomplished in Christ Jesus on my behalf in light of this particular mystery:*

Original Sin unleashed upon the world an evolution of rage in the overwhelming grief of divorcing one's self from the *ecstasy of intimacy* with God and each other. This is Satan's rage which by choice we made our own. In this rage, human relationships are violated at every level, making sin's gravest trauma that of abandonment and loneliness. There is no greater suffering Christ Jesus endured than in becoming for us the totality of that abandonment and lovelessness. In freely absorbing our sins in His Sacred Heart, He is cut-off from experiencing the Father's love, and from those depths forgives us, mending permanently the communion of love that was our birthright with the Trinity and each other.

✳ *I now pray to understand how the truth of this universal Mystery uniquely applies to my own Sacred Story:*

How do I selflessly carry the legacy of abandonment caused by sin in my life, my family and my relationships? How do I call upon the Father's mercy when I endure the loss of communion's perfect intimacy in my interior life, my life with God and in my efforts to create loving relationships with others? What is the darkest place in my heart Christ Jesus desires to visit so He hold forever in His pierced Sacred Heart; sin's legacy of abandonment in my own? How do I model Christ Jesus' forgiveness in my own life?

✳ *I now examine my own life in light of how I have or have not lived up to the ideal to which the Mystery invites me to model:*

Do I abandon those unable to love me the way I want? How do I violate my relationship with myself; with God; with others? How do I avoid letting Christ Jesus penetrate the darkness in my heart? Do I carry graciously my measure of abandonment and loneliness that is the sad inheritance of humanity's rejecting God? Do I refuse to forgive family members, friends or intimates for any reason whatsoever? Do I refuse to ask God's grace to forgive those who violated or broke trust with me in any way whatsoever? Am I grateful to Christ for ending the curse of separation from divine intimacy?

✳ *I close with a prayer of thanksgiving to Christ for walking the path of the Mystery in complete fidelity to the Father's will. I pray that I can be inspired by the Mystery's high ideal once again and that I too, can more faithfully live it in my own Sacred Story.*

Dear Lord Jesus, in your forsakenness on the cross you enter into communion with any and every one abused or abandoned by sin's isolation and lovelessness. You end the despair of abandonment to restore the communion we were destined to share with the Trinity and each other. Dear Jesus, may I have the desire to emulate you in sharing the abandonment of those broken by sin's rage and violence. May I better understand and be forever grateful for your love in accepting the full measure of sin's lovelessness. You are the Lord of Glory. Amen!

THE MYSTERIES OF GLORY

THE RESURRECTION

THE ASCENSION

THE DESCENT OF THE HOLY SPIRIT

THE ASSUMPTION OF MARY

THE CORONATION OF MARY

These Mysteries are generally prayed on

Wednesday, Saturday & Sunday

THE RESURRECTION

But at daybreak on the first day of the week they took the spices they had prepared and went to the tomb. They found the stone rolled away from the tomb; but when they entered, they did not find the body of the Lord Jesus. While they were puzzling over this, behold, two men in dazzling garments appeared to them. They were terrified and bowed their faces to the ground. They said to them, "Why do you seek the living one among the dead? He is not here, but he has been raised. Remember what he said to you while he was still in Galilee, that the Son of Man must be handed over to sinners and be crucified, and rise on the third day." Now that very day two of them were going to a village seven miles from Jerusalem called Emmaus, and they were conversing about all the things that had occurred. And it happened that while they were conversing and debating, Jesus himself drew near and walked with them, but their eyes were prevented from recognizing him. And he said to them, "Oh, how foolish you are! How slow of heart to believe all that the prophets spoke! Was it not necessary that the Messiah should suffer these things and enter into his glory?" *(Lk 24: 1-6, 13-16, 25-26)*

THE HEART OF THE MYSTERY

✳ *I speak the mystery in my heart allowing its truth to shape my time of prayer.*

Christ Jesus, by your glorious resurrection the Father recreates the cosmos and redeems human nature, revealing anew humankind as the purpose and most precious gift of God's creation.

✳ *I now ponder what God has accomplished in Christ Jesus on my behalf in light of this particular mystery:*

Lord Jesus, sin destroyed our human nature crafted in the Divine image and likeness. In your resurrection, human nature is restored and I see once again my supreme value as a beloved child of God. In Your resurrection I see how sin's most grievous wounds can become my source of joy and hope. In Your resurrection I see that death cannot prevent the communion of eternal love with you and all the saints of God, established by the Trinity as my birthright.

✳ *I now pray to understand how the truth of this universal Mystery uniquely applies to my own Sacred Story:*

I pray to understand how my human nature wounded by sin is restored in Christ. What spiritual, psychological, physical and mental deficits in my life do I want Christ to heal? I can rejoice because the Father sees my broken human nature through Jesus' glory as perfect and inviolate. Because of Jesus' supreme sacrifice and resurrection, I can be certain that humanity is the height of God's creation and its ultimate purpose.

✳ *I now examine my own life in light of how I have or have not lived up to the ideal to which the Mystery invites me to model:*

Do I stand with the Church as she tries to protect the truth about human nature when culture denies it? Do I surrender to discouragement when I reflect on my brokenness? Am I tempted to surrender to the brokenness of my human nature as my true identity? Do I pray for the hope, patience and faith I need in awaiting the day of my own rebirth to eternal life? Do I keep my eyes on Christ's glorious wounds and his triumphant resurrection so as not to despair? Am I grateful to Christ for healing the wounds of my human nature?

✳ *I close with a prayer of thanksgiving to Christ for walking the path of the Mystery in complete fidelity to the Father's will. I pray that I can be inspired by the Mystery's high ideal once again and that I too, can more faithfully live it in my own Sacred Story.*

Dear Lord Jesus, You have restored my dignity as a child of God by carrying in your body the cruelest violence and darkest despair by which human nature is oppressed. You have triumphed over human nature's enemy and become the first born of the dead. Your resurrection commences the new heavens and the new earth that is both our lasting joy and your own. May I always keep my eyes on you and never lose hope due to sin's wounds in my life. May I not succumb to despair over the contempt this present age holds for human nature made in the Divine image and likeness. May I always see in You the Truth of my human nature and know the hope you give me by burying my wounds in your own. Amen!

THE ASCENSION OF THE LORD

He presented himself alive to them by many proofs after he had suffered, appearing to them during forty days and speaking about the kingdom of God. While meeting with them, he enjoined them not to depart from Jerusalem, but to wait for "the promise of the Father about which you have heard me speak; for John baptized with water, but in a few days you will be baptized with the holy Spirit." When they had gathered together they asked him, "Lord, are you at this time going to restore the kingdom to Israel?" He answered them, "It is not for you to know the times or seasons that the Father has established by his own authority. But you will receive power when the holy Spirit comes upon you, and you will be my witnesses in Jerusalem, throughout Judea and Samaria, and to the ends of the earth." When he had said this, as they were looking on, he was lifted up, and a cloud took him from their sight." *(Acts 1: 6-9)*

THE HEART OF THE MYSTERY

✳ *I speak the mystery in my heart allowing its truth to shape my time of prayer.*

Christ your Ascension inaugurates our vocation as Your co-laborers in humanity's reconciliation with the Father, and thus you exult us even beyond our privileged place in Paradise.

✳ *I now ponder what God has accomplished in Christ Jesus on my behalf in light of this particular mystery:*

In Christ's Ascension, the Father glorifies the Redeemer of human nature. In this act, the Father also entrusts the Church and her faithful with the glorious work of universal reconciliation. More than a loving parent surrenders authority and responsibility to a beloved child, Christ Jesus freely lavishes on us a portion of His redemptive mission so we can share in the Father's glorification of the Son.

✳ *I now pray to understand how the truth of this universal Mystery uniquely applies to my own Sacred Story:*

I pray to know and accept my highest vocation with Christ in his redemption of the human race. I ask to be given the grace to witness to Christ in all my thoughts words and deeds. I pray for strength to accept the privilege of responsibility Christ Jesus entrusts to me, that I might produce fruit that endures to eternity. I pray to believe that my life has ultimate value and that every suffering I endure for Him has a role in the salvation of the world. I anticipate the time when Christ will bring me before His Father in the company of redeemed humanity to reveal and honor my role in His salvific work"

✳ *I now examine my own life in light of how I have or have not lived up to the ideal to which the Mystery invites me to model:*

Do I take seriously my central vocation as a Christian to give witness to Christ in every thought, word and deed? Do I take time to daily discern God's call of how I might better serve Christ Jesus? Have I placed other vocations, unworthy of my dignity as a redeemed child of God, ahead of my Christian vocation? Do I work for glory in this life or for the glory of the life to come? Am I grateful for Christ's entrustment to me of sharing in his redemptive mission?

✳ *I close with a prayer of thanksgiving to Christ for walking the path of the Mystery in complete fidelity to the Father's will. I pray that I can be inspired by the Mystery's high ideal once again and that I too, can more faithfully live it in my own Sacred Story.*

Dear Lord Jesus, the Father glories in Your triumphant sacrifice of Love and blesses the work of reconciliation that you have given to the Church and her faithful. Thank you for restoring my dignity and giving me a vocation that will produce fruit enduring to eternity. Thank you for inviting me to your friendship, with all the holy ones who follow your call. May I listen daily for your voice in my heart so that I might serve you more faithfully in all I think, say and do. Amen!

THE DESCENT OF THE HOLY SPIRIT

When they entered the city they went to the upper room where they were staying, Peter and John and James and Andrew, Philip and Thomas, Bartholomew and Matthew, James son of Alphaeus, Simon the Zealot, and Judas son of James. All these devoted themselves with one accord to prayer, together with some women, and Mary the mother of Jesus, and his brothers. When the time for Pentecost was fulfilled, they were all in one place together. And suddenly there came from the sky a noise like a strong driving wind, and it filled the entire house in which they were. Then there appeared to them tongues as of fire, which parted and came to rest on each one of them. And they were all filled with the holy Spirit and began to speak in different tongues, as the Spirit enabled them to proclaim." *(Acts 1: 13-14; 2: 1-4)*

✳

THE HEART OF THE MYSTERY

✳ *I speak the mystery in my heart allowing its truth to shape my time of prayer.*

Holy Trinity, You bestow Your Love on Mary and the disciples, creating a community of reconciliation that conquers sin's legacy of abandonment, isolation and death.

✳ *I now ponder what God has accomplished in Christ Jesus on my behalf in light of this particular mystery:*

Christ Jesus, the Holy Spirit is the fire that transforms Mary and the disciples into Your Body the Church. You mission her to spread the Good News of forgiveness. This mercy is Your gift of reconciling love, to end human nature's abandonment. The communion of believers under Peter will triumph in that mission, no matter their weakness or shame because You promise to be with the Church until the end of the age (Mt 28: 20). In the Church you give me a home here on earth and the sure hope of a lasting kingdom in the world to come. You baptize me as a friend and disciple, a beloved member of Your Body, to spread your Good News to the ends of the earth.

✳ *I now pray to understand how the truth of this universal Mystery uniquely applies to my own Sacred Story:*

Jesus, Your Holy Spirit present in the Church is my promise of forgiveness, no matter the gravity of my sins. You promise me that where sin abounds, Your grace will be even more abundant (Rm 5: 20). You invite me to frequently receive your reconciling love and in my joy, be a living example of your reconciliation in all I do and with all I meet. You give me a mission of more value than the gold of all empires past or present. You have given me a holy family of brothers and sisters to help me be faithful to your call. In Your Church, you give me shelter from Satan's power until I am safely with you in the communion of saints.

✳ *I now examine my own life in light of how I have or have not lived up to the ideal to which the Mystery invites me to model:*

Do I call upon the Holy Spirit daily for the grace and assistance I need in my life's mission? Have I anchored my life in the communion of the Church where I can grow in faith, hope and love? Do I faithfully eat and drink of the Body and Blood of Christ in the Holy Sacrifice of the Mass? Do I call upon the Holy Spirit to understand my sins and their consequences? Do I faithfully receive the sacrament of Reconciliation to be washed clean by the blood Christ shed on my behalf? Do realize that the greatest gift I can give Christ Jesus is my sins so He can reconcile me with the Father? Do I stand with the Body of Christ against the works of Satan in the world today? Do I call upon Mary the mother of Jesus to aid both me and the Church in the mission of reconciliation?

✳ *I close with a prayer of thanksgiving to Christ and Mary for walking the path of the Mystery in complete fidelity to the Father's will. I pray that I can be inspired by the Mystery's high ideal once again and that I too, can more faithfully live it in my own Sacred Story.*

Dear Lord Jesus, thank you for the gift of your Holy Spirit in the Church and in my life. Thank you for honoring the Blessed Virgin's devotion at your cross, the first of all the disciples. Thank you for giving me a home and a mission, by the gift of the Church. Thank you for your fidelity to me and the Church, to be with us until the end of the age, no matter the failure or shame incurred. Thank you for your gift of reconciling Love. Let me grow daily in your Love, so I can be, with my brothers and sisters in Christ, a true disciple, friend and a model of your reconciling Love. Amen.

THE ASSUMPTION OF MARY

And Mary said: "My soul proclaims the greatness of the Lord; my spirit rejoices in God my savior. For he has looked upon his handmaid's lowliness; behold, from now on will all ages call me blessed. The Mighty One has done great things for me, and holy is his name. His mercy is from age to age to those who fear him. He has shown might with his arm, dispersed the arrogant of mind and heart. He has thrown down the rulers from their thrones but lifted up the lowly. The hungry he has filled with good things; the rich he has sent away empty. He has helped Israel his servant, remembering his mercy, according to his promise to our fathers, to Abraham and to his descendants forever." *(Lk 1: 46-55)*

THE HEART OF THE MYSTERY

✳ *I speak the mystery in my heart allowing its truth to shape my time of prayer.*

Blessed Mary, your Assumption body and soul into glory without bodily corruption signifies your role as the highest honor of our race and prefigures the restoration of our own human nature even beyond its former glory, in and through Christ Jesus.

✳ *I now ponder what God has accomplished in Christ Jesus and Mary on my behalf in light of this particular mystery:*

Christ Jesus, you hallowed the Virgin Mary at her conception and freed her from sin's disease. She is the first to love God with her whole heart and her whole being (Dt 10: 12-13). She freely said "YES" to God in her life, even to bearing in her womb the Son of the Eternal Father. Mary's obedience and her complete "YES" preserved her human nature from sin's division and so she passed from Earth to Heaven, her body and soul as inviolate as on the day of her conception. Mary's Assumption heralds the renewal of our body and soul made in the Divine image and gives witness to the Truth about God, human nature and His creation of humankind made through and for Christ Jesus.

✳ *I now pray to understand how the truth of this universal Mystery uniquely applies to my own Sacred Story:*

I pray Mary that you help me understand how marvelous a being I am, body and soul, made in the Divine image and likeness. Help me believe that my human nature with its holy longings broken by sin, will one day be restored inviolate to eternal vigor, beauty and wholeness. Your Assumption foreshadows for me the physical resurrection of the elect and the promise of eternal ecstasy for those who cooperate with your Son's mission. Increase my desire to be counted among them.

✳ *I now examine my own life in light of how I have or have not lived up to the ideal to which the Mystery invites me to model:*

Do I call upon the Blessed Mother regularly when I experience the sorrows of this life? Do I let myself be overcome with grief rather than seek the intercession of the Mother of Sorrows, who has been raised to glory to comfort to the lowly and broken of the world? Do I marvel at Mary's holiness and see it as the icon of what Christ Jesus invites me to share? Do I daily say "YES" to Christ in all my thoughts, words and deeds so that my sorrows in life due to my own sin may diminish? Am I grateful to God for choosing Mary as the Mother of Jesus, and giving her to me as Mother?

✳ *I close with a prayer of thanksgiving to Christ and Mary for walking the path of the Mystery in complete fidelity to the Father's will. I pray that I can be inspired by the Mystery's high ideal once again and that I too, can more faithfully live it in my own Sacred Story.*

Dear Lord Jesus, you exalt the Blessed Mother in her Assumption and reveal not only her glory as the handmaid of the Trinity but also the image of hope to which I am called. Let me never doubt that my broken human nature will be restored by your grace, especially when life's trials seem too much to bear. In those times, grant me the grace to turn to Mary for her help in overcoming the darkness of my own sin and the temptations of human nature's enemy. Mary, bring me comfort and hope until I am safely with you and the Lord's elect in the Kingdom of the Father. Amen!

THE CORONATION OF MARY

A great sign appeared in the sky, a woman clothed with the sun, with the moon under her feet, and on her head a crown of twelve stars. She was with child and wailed aloud in pain as she labored to give birth. Then another sign appeared in the sky; it was a huge red dragon, with seven heads and ten horns, and on its heads were seven diadems. Its tail swept away a third of the stars in the sky and hurled them down to the earth. Then the dragon stood before the woman about to give birth, to devour her child when she gave birth. The huge dragon, the ancient serpent, who is called the Devil and Satan, who deceived the whole world, was thrown down to earth, and its angels were thrown down with it. Then I heard a loud voice in heaven say: "Now have salvation and power come, and the kingdom of our God and the authority of his Anointed. For the accuser of our brothers is cast out, who accuses them before our God day and night. *(Rev 12:1-4; 9-10)*

THE HEART OF THE MYSTERY

 I speak the mystery in my heart allowing its truth to shape my time of prayer.

Dearest Mary you countered the enemy's dark powers with total obedience and humility, and for your victory are crowned by the Blessed Trinity as Queen of Heaven and Queen of the World to Come.

 I now ponder what God has accomplished in Christ Jesus and Mary on my behalf in light of this particular mystery:

"As Christ Jesus, so the Blessed Mother surrendered completely to the Father's will. An innocent victim of injustice like her Son, she absorbed in her Immaculate Heart the violent hate of the arrogant. Never seeking retribution but trusting in the Father, Mary makes evident that humility will conquer the power of ego. Her humility and obedience will never be matched and for this she is exulted with the highest honors accorded to any of our race.

 I now pray to understand how this universal Mystery of the cosmos uniquely applies to my own Sacred Story:

I am invited to believe that humble obedience to Christ and His Church is my shield against the corruption of sin and the world's dark powers. I ask to understand what violence and hate in my own life I need to confront with silence and forgiveness. I consider how I am tempted to meet power with power, so I can learn better where to grow in humility and trust. I measure my thoughts, words and deeds not for the accolades of this present age, but the age to come, when Christ acknowledges His beloved before the heavenly court with His Blessed Mother.

✳ *I now examine my own life in light of how I have or have not lived up to the ideal to which the Mystery invites me to model:*

Do I walk the path of humility and obedience with Christ and His Church? Do I believe in a heavenly reward for living a life of humility and obedience? Do I succumb to meeting violence with violence, instead of absorbing in my own heart the hatred centered on me or my beliefs? Do I seek retribution for the injustices visited upon me or do I trust in the Father's justice? Is the balance of my life measured by selflessness or selfishness? Do I conduct my affairs to earn eternal rewards or work for the praise of my contemporaries? Do I anticipate the consolation of Christ honoring me before his Father, the Blessed Mother and the entire heavenly court?

✳ *I close with a prayer of thanksgiving to Christ and Mary for walking the path of the Mystery in complete fidelity to the Father's will. I pray that I can be inspired by the Mystery's high ideal once again and that I too, can more faithfully live it in my own Sacred Story.*

I thank you Holy Trinity for choosing a human person for so exalted a mission in the salvation of the human race. In Blessed Mary's victory and coronation I understand more fully the path you have set before me and the honor you seek to give me in Your Kingdom. Holy Trinity, I ask your grace to choose your will in all my thoughts, words and deeds. Grant me the grace to work for heaven's glory and so be a full disciple with Mary in that Kingdom of joy, hope and peace that you desire for all your children. Amen!

THE MYSTERIES OF LIGHT[12]

THE BAPTISM IN THE JORDAN

THE WEDDING AT CANA

THE PROCLAMATION OF THE KINGDOM

THE TRANSFIGURATION

THE INSTITUTION OF THE EUCHARIST

These Mysteries are generally prayed on

Thursday

The Baptism of the Lord in the Jordan

Then Jesus came from Galilee to John at the Jordan to be baptized by him. John tried to prevent him, saying, "I need to be baptized by you, and yet you are coming to me?" Jesus said to him in reply, "Allow it now, for thus it is fitting for us to fulfill all righteousness." Then he allowed him. After Jesus was baptized, he came up from the water and behold, the heavens were opened for him, and he saw the Spirit of God descending like a dove and coming upon him. And a voice came from the heavens, saying, "This is my beloved Son, with whom I am well pleased." *(Mt 3: 13-17)*

THE HEART OF THE MYSTERY

✳ *I speak the mystery in my heart allowing its truth to shape my time of prayer.*

Lord Jesus, you are the head, the first our race, to receive the baptism of the Father and His outpouring of grace for the mission to free enslaved human nature from the power of Satan."

✳ *I now ponder what God has accomplished in Christ Jesus and Mary on my behalf in light of this particular mystery:*

The Father anoints Jesus to begin his glorious mission. The Father is well pleased by Jesus' full embrace of the cost of glory (Mt 3: 17). The anointing drives Jesus to the desert, the place of encounter with sin's chaos in the history of the human race. It is there He comes face to face with Satan, the ruler of this age. In rejecting Satan's three temptations, Jesus restores the poverty, chastity and obedience that humankind lost in the Original Sin. Jesus' baptism empowers our baptism and shapes the mission we are invited to share with Christ under the full blessing and delight of the Father.

✳ *I now pray to understand how the truth of this universal Mystery uniquely applies to my own Sacred Story:*

Do I understand that my baptism empowers me with grace to confront the disorder and sin in my own history? What deserts of human culture has my baptism empowered me to enter and share in Jesus' renewal of poverty, chastity and obedience? Have I seen myself as the chosen and beloved of the Father when I accept the baptismal mission of my Faith?

✳ *I now examine my own life in light of how I have or have not lived up to the ideal to which the Mystery invites me to model:*

Have I resisted the call of my baptism to share in Jesus' mission in the world? What places in the desert of my own heart have I feared to tread or allowed Jesus to enter? What are my particular temptations against poverty, chastity and obedience? To which periphery of society, far from my comfort zone, is Christ inviting me? ? Have I resisted the call to bring His salvific message of joy and reconciliation to these places?

✳ *I close with a prayer of thanksgiving to Christ and Mary for walking the path of the Mystery in complete fidelity to the Father's will. I pray that I can be inspired by the Mystery's high ideal once again and that I too, can more faithfully live it in my own Sacred Story.*

Lord Jesus Christ, thank you for accepting the Father's baptism and his mission to rescue human nature from tragedy and death. Thank you for allowing me to join your mission. May I too hear the Father say of my labor with you, that He is "well pleased May I have the courage to enter the desert of my heart for the joy you wish to bring to me. Calm my fears of journeying to the peripheries of my own heart and the hearts of your people, so the Gospel joy of poverty, chastity and obedience may reach those most in need of Your Saving Grace. Amen!

THE WEDDING FEAST AT CANA

On the third day there was a wedding in Cana in Galilee, and the mother of Jesus was there. Jesus and his disciples were also invited to the wedding. When the wine ran short, the mother of Jesus said to him, "They have no wine." And Jesus said to her, "Woman, how does your concern affect me? My hour has not yet come." His mother said to the servers, "Do whatever he tells you." Now there were six stone water jars there for Jewish ceremonial washings, each holding twenty to thirty gallons. Jesus told them, "Fill the jars with water." So they filled them to the brim. Then he told them, "Draw some out now and take it to the headwaiter." So they took it. And when the headwaiter tasted the water that had become wine, without knowing where it came from (although the servers who had drawn the water knew), the headwaiter called the bridegroom and said to him, "Everyone serves good wine first, and then when people have drunk freely, an inferior one; but you have kept the good wine until now." Jesus did this as the beginning of his signs in Cana in Galilee and so

revealed his glory, and his disciples began to believe in him.
(Jn 2: 1-11)

THE HEART OF THE MYSTERY

 I speak the mystery in my heart allowing its truth to shape my time of prayer.

Christ Jesus, You signify the beginning of your mission by Your outpouring of grace, the new wine of the kingdom, to consecrate woman and man joined in fruitful marriage.

 I now ponder what God has accomplished in Christ Jesus and Mary on my behalf in light of this particular mystery:

The miracle at Cana renews God's plan for man and woman, joined in fruitful covenant love; an image of the Trinity. Cana is Christ's holy sign that marriage is the anchor of human culture and the bright promise of society renewed in God's image. The miracle at Cana demonstrates the rightful expression of sexuality's gift for which God created human nature. The miracle at Cana is the assurance for all those married in Christ of His fidelity. It is the outpouring of grace He promises for couples to persevere in their covenant and so secure love's eternal promise for them and their children.

 I now pray to understand how the truth of this universal Mystery uniquely applies to my own Sacred Story:

What is my desire to share in the outpouring of grace Cana

signifies? How does it call forth from me a renewal of marital love; the icon of the Trinity? How am I called to protect the sacredness of human sexuality, according to the plan of the Father? How does Christ ask me to be renewed in my human nature so that, as male or female, I may more authentically express in my own life God's plan for holy matrimony? What does Christ ask of me in protecting the sacredness of marriage as the anchor of civilization, the hope of children and the future of the human race?

✳ *I examine my own life in light of how I have or have not lived up to the ideal to which the Mystery invites me to model:*

In my marriage, do I renew with daily prayer the covenant God has sanctified? Do I stand with Christ in the Church to shelter the sacredness of marriage? Do I ask God for the courage to honestly examine my sexual desires to discern where they stray from the laws of Christ as taught by the Church? Do I receive frequent confession to be forgiven when I surrender to my lusts? Do I teach the beauty of chastity before marriage? Do I celebrate procreation as the very apex of human participation in God's creative act, freely bestowed on woman and man as the one gift and blessing not broken by Original Sin?

✳ *I close with a prayer of thanksgiving to Christ and Mary for walking the path of the Mystery in complete fidelity to the Father's will. I pray that I can be inspired by the Mystery's high ideal once again and that I too, can more faithfully live it in my own Sacred Story.*

Lord Jesus and Blessed Mary, thank you for the gift of Cana; the new wine celebrating the renewal of human nature in the covenant of marital love. Intercede on behalf of all married people for the fidelity and fruitfulness of their love. Christ, help those broken by infidelity to find your healing graces. Please mend their hearts. May you guide all children to your eternal kingdom no matter the circumstances of their birth. Christ Jesus, help me daily to grow more fully conformed in my own vocation to the image of love the covenant of marriage signifies. Please renew all families with the superabundance of grace outpoured at the miracle at the Wedding Feast at Cana. Amen!

The Proclamation of the Kingdom

And raising his eyes toward his disciples he said: "Blessed are you who are poor, for the kingdom of God is yours. Blessed are you who are now hungry, for you will be satisfied. Blessed are you who are now weeping, for you will laugh. Blessed are you when people hate you, and when they exclude and insult you, and denounce your name as evil on account of the Son of Man. Rejoice and leap for joy on that day! Behold, your reward will be great in heaven. For their ancestors treated the prophets in the same way. But woe to you who are rich, for you have received your consolation. But woe to you who are filled now, for you will be hungry. Woe to you who laugh now, for you will grieve and weep. Woe to you when all speak well of you, for their ancestors treated the false prophets in this way. *(Lk 6: 20-26)*

When Jesus finished giving these commands to his twelve disciples, he went away from that place to teach and to preach in their towns. When John heard in prison of the works of the Messiah, he sent his disciples to him with this question, "Are you the one who is to come, or should we look for another?" Jesus said to them in reply, "Go and tell John what you hear and see: the blind regain their sight, the lame walk, lepers are cleansed, the deaf hear, the dead are raised, and the poor have the good news proclaimed to them. And blessed is the one who takes no offense at me. *(Mt 11:1-6)*

THE HEART OF THE MYSTERY

✴ I speak the mystery in my heart allowing its truth to shape my time of prayer.

Christ Jesus, Your proclamation of God's Kingdom inaugurates the eternal reign of righteousness that will shame and supplant every empire, government or system of temporal power the world has built.

✴ I now ponder what God has accomplished in Christ Jesus and Mary on my behalf in light of this particular mystery:

Jesus Christ, the Proclamation of God's Kingdom assures the transience of every worldly power. For your Kingdom is not of this world's design but of the Father's. You are the GOOD NEWS of God's nearness to the Chosen, and Israel's hope for salvation is now our own. Your message of hope overturns the power of the arrogant to lift high the poor in spirit. The humble and those who suffer persecution in Your name are the most exulted in Your new reign. You stand with Your Church as a bulwark against the powers of destruction. You give us courage to shun the world's glories and all its empty honors, for a lasting place in Your eternal Kingdom.

✳ *I now pray to understand how the truth of this universal Mystery uniquely applies to my own Sacred Story:*

I am called to proclaim the Kingdom with my own life and to call others to conversion by my own example. What is my vocation in this proclamation today? What is my deepest aspiration for helping the blind see, the lame walk, the imprisoned be freed and the poor hear the good news preached to them? What is my ideal in following the humble example of Christ, as my model in confronting the world's powers? What divisions am I called to heal, by working for reconciliation in all that I do? How is the Lord freeing me from the temptations of worldly riches, honors, and power, to live my life for the rewards of an everlasting Kingdom?

✳ *I now examine my own life in light of how I have or have not lived up to the ideal to which the Mystery invites me to model:*

Do I labor with Christ in proclaiming his Kingdom? Do I help others believe the Kingdom's values for the poor, the lame, the blind and the imprisoned, by my words and my example? Where do I take offense at the Church's proclamation of the Kingdom? When do I fail to announce the Kingdom because I am offended at the price of the proclamation? Do stand with and pray for those who are persecuted for proclaiming the Kingdom of Christ?

✳ *I close with a prayer of thanksgiving to Christ and Mary for walking the path of the Mystery in complete fidelity to the Father's will. I pray that I can be inspired by the Mystery's high ideal once again and that I too, can more faithfully live it in my own Sacred Story:*

Lord Jesus, thank you for establishing the new Kingdom for your Church to build the civilization of love as a light for all victims oppressed by worldly powers. May we always be grateful and faithful to the Church as she assumes the full mantle of her glory as your Body on earth, in proclaiming the Good News of salvation to all peoples. Always make my life a living example of that proclamation so I can bring hope to all I meet. Amen!

THE TRANSFIGURATION OF THE LORD

After six days Jesus took Peter, James, and John his brother, and led them up a high mountain by themselves. And he was transfigured before them; his face shone like the sun and his clothes became white as light. And behold, Moses and Elijah appeared to them, conversing with him. Then Peter said to Jesus in reply, "Lord, it is good that we are here. If you wish, I will make three tents here, one for you, one for Moses, and one for Elijah." While he was still speaking, behold, a bright cloud cast a shadow over them, then from the cloud came a voice that said, "This is my beloved Son, with whom I am well pleased; listen to him." When the disciples heard this, they fell prostrate and were very much afraid. But Jesus came and touched them, saying, "Rise, and do not be afraid." And when the disciples raised their eyes, they saw no one else but Jesus alone. *(Mt 17: 1-8)*

THE HEART OF THE MYSTERY

✳ I speak the mystery in my heart allowing its truth to shape my time of prayer.

Lord Jesus, your transfiguration reveals to your disciples and all people that You are the Son of Man, the glory of the Father, and the glory that will belong to the children of God who follow You.

✳ I now ponder what God has accomplished in Christ Jesus and Mary on my behalf in light of this particular mystery:

Lord Christ Jesus, you surrendered your heavenly glory becoming our slave to suffer the cost of our sins. Your obedience to the Father, in humbly accepting the plan for our salvation, hid your true glory from the powers and principalities of the age. Yet the Father heralds you as the one to whom every knee will bow (Phil 2: 2-7). Those who have the eyes of faith and the innocence of children see the hope of glory in Your splendor. In Your Father's exultation, we see our own future glory.

✳ I now pray to understand how the truth of this universal Mystery uniquely applies to my own Sacred Story:

I am invited to believe that the glory of our human race and the delight of the Father is concealed from the wise. It is visible to me when I humbly submit to the Father. I am invited to see the glory of Christ hidden in my own human nature and in my life. I am invited to believe that my limitations of sin and darkness conceal an eternal being of infinite beauty and grace beheld in Christ, before the Father of all. I am invited to hear my Father in heaven say of me, here is my beloved in whom I take delight.

✳ *I now examine my own life in light of how I have or have not lived up to the ideal to which the Mystery invites me to model:*

Do I seek my own fame or the Father's will, waiting for Him to reveal His glory in me? Do I cultivate the innocence of a child so that I can behold Jesus as my Savior and the Light of the World? Do I disbelieve the glory to be mine in Christ because of the sin, frailty or persecution I bear in my body? When I doubt Jesus' glory, do I ask the Father to reveal Him in a way that helps me believe? Do I lack gratitude for the times the Father has shown me Jesus' glory in my own history? Do I lose hope in God for the glory of the Church as the Body of Christ, when she suffers persecution and weakness?

✳ *I close with a prayer of thanksgiving to Christ and Mary for walking the path of the Mystery in complete fidelity to the Father's will. I pray that I can be inspired by the Mystery's high ideal once again and that I too, can more faithfully live it in my own Sacred Story:*

Dear Lord Jesus, I bend my knee at the Father's exultation of Your obedience and humility. Thank you for showing the innocent Your glory, shared with the Father since the world's foundation. Increase my desire for innocence. Make me a better disciple by granting me the grace to more fully conform my life to the obedience and humility You modeled. Help me to believe that I might fully share in Your glory in the Kingdom of the Father for all eternity. Amen!

THE INSTITUTION OF THE EUCHARIST

When the hour came, he took his place at table with the apostles. He said to them, "I have eagerly desired to eat this Passover with you before I suffer, for, I tell you, I shall not eat it [again] until there is fulfillment in the kingdom of God." Then he took a cup, gave thanks, and said, "Take this and share it among yourselves; for I tell you [that] from this time on I shall not drink of the fruit of the vine until the kingdom of God comes." Then he took the bread, said the blessing, broke it, and gave it to them, saying, "This is my body, which will be given for you; do this in memory of me." And likewise the cup after they had eaten, saying, "This cup is the new covenant in my blood, which will be shed for you." *(Lk 22:14-20)*

So when he had washed their feet [and] put his garments back on and reclined at table again, he said to them, "Do you realize what I have done for you? You call me 'teacher' and 'master,' and rightly so, for indeed I am. If I, therefore, the master and teacher, have washed your feet, you ought to wash one another's feet. I have given you a model to follow, so that as I have done for you, you should also do. This is my commandment: love one another as I love you. No one has greater love than this, to lay down one's life for one's friends. You are my friends if you do what I command you." *(Jn 13: 12-15; 12-14)*

THE HEART OF THE MYSTERY

✳ *I speak the mystery in my heart allowing its truth to shape my time of prayer.*

Dear Jesus, the sacrificial gift of the Eucharist is Your full divine and human Presence, and our sustenance for eternal life; Your *ecstasy of eternal intimacy* with those created through You and for You.

✳ *I now ponder what God has accomplished in Christ Jesus and Mary on my behalf in light of this particular mystery:*

The Eucharist is Christ and His sacrifice of love made present in history for all time. He is the grain of wheat that dies, falling into the ground to become the spring of our salvation and the foundation of a new heavens and the new earth. He has become our Bread of Life, the never-ending gift of His Presence to the

Church, His Body on earth. The Eucharist is His promise to remain with us, body and soul, until the end of the age. The Eucharist is His Paschal Longing; the ecstasy of intimacy He has sought with His beloved since the tragedy of Original Sin. Those receiving the Eucharist are intimate with Christ and through Him, mystically connected with everyone who has lived, is living, or will live, and the whole of creation—because everything that has been, is, or will be was created "through Him and for Him.

✳ *I now pray to understand how the truth of this universal Mystery uniquely applies to my own Sacred Story:*

The Holy Eucharist is my presence at Calvary's eternal gift of sacrificing love. It is the Divine Majesty's gift to be forever intimate with me. The Holy Eucharist is Christ's longing to enter my wounds, touch my flesh and become in me the healing remedy for my eternal life. In the Holy Eucharist, Christ invites me to the new communion of fraternal love in his Body the Church, the fountain of grace for the whole human race. In the Holy Eucharist, Christ invites me to remain in Him, as He remains in me. In the Holy Eucharist I have communion through Him with all my loved ones who have passed from this life. In the Holy Eucharist and the Church, the Body of Christ, I have assurance I will never again be abandoned or separated from Christ's love. (Rm 8: 18-39).

✳ *I now examine my own life in light of how I have or have not lived up to the ideal to which the Mystery invites me to model:*

Do I cherish the gift of the Holy Eucharist and do I let Christ cherish me and save me in this Holy Communion? Do I frequently partake of the Holy Eucharist and take time to properly prepare, particularly regarding grave sin? Do I see my sisters and brothers in the Eucharistic Body of Christ as worth dying for? Does the reconciliation offered in the Eucharist stir me to labor for unity in all my relationships and communities? Do I share with others the truth of Christ's presence in the Eucharist? Do I see my participation in Holy Mass as the promise and foretaste of the communion of saints in the Eternal Banquet of Christ and His Father?

✳ *I close with a prayer of thanksgiving to Christ and Mary for walking the path of the Mystery in complete fidelity to the Father's will. I pray that I can be inspired by the Mystery's high ideal once again and that I too, can more faithfully live it in my own Sacred Story:*

Lord Jesus, my heart rejoices at Your loving presence in the gift of the Holy Eucharist. Thank You for ending my estrangement from God and reconciling me to the Father. Thank you for making me one with You in the Church, the Body of Christ on earth. By my frequent reception of your Holy Eucharist, may I hunger and thirst more each day for the Eternal Banquet, the heritage promised to your faithful in the Kingdom to come. Amen!

MY SACRED STORY ROSARY

This book concludes with *your* chapter called, "My Sacred Story Rosary." Learn the Mysteries of Sacred Story Rosary "by heart," as I have presented them. Pray them for a month or two by remembering a shorter version of each five-fold reflection presented in the preceding chapter for each Mystery.

After a month or two praying Sacred Story Rosary, concisely summarize each of the twenty Mystery's five reflections in your *own* words based on your personal history and the ways you experience your call as a Christian in your daily life with the Lord.

When you pray the Rosary in the future, you will have a way to reflect on and pray about the most fundamental truths of the cosmos in light of your own unique *Sacred Story*.

THE ANNUNCIATION TO MARY

✳ I speak the mystery in my heart allowing its truth to shape my time of prayer.

✳ I now ponder what God has accomplished in Christ Jesus and Mary on my behalf in light of this particular mystery:

✳ I now pray to understand how the truth of this universal Mystery uniquely applies to my own Sacred Story:

✳ I examine my own life in light of how I have or have not lived up to the ideal to which the Mystery invites me to model:

✳ I close with a prayer of thanksgiving to Christ and Mary for walking the path of the Mystery in complete fidelity to the Father's will. I pray that I can be inspired by the Mystery's high ideal once again and that I too, can more faithfully live it in my own Sacred Story.

THE VISITATION OF MARY

✳ I speak the mystery in my heart allowing its truth to shape my time of prayer.

✳ I now ponder what God has accomplished in Christ Jesus and Mary on my behalf in light of this particular mystery:

✳ I now pray to understand how the truth of this universal Mystery uniquely applies to my own Sacred Story:

✳ I examine my own life in light of how I have or have not lived up to the ideal to which the Mystery invites me to model:

✳ I close with a prayer of thanksgiving to Christ and Mary for walking the path of the Mystery in complete fidelity to the Father's will. I pray that I can be inspired by the Mystery's high ideal once again and that I too, can more faithfully live it in my own Sacred Story.

THE NATIVITY OF THE LORD

✳ I speak the mystery in my heart allowing its truth to shape my time of prayer.

✳ I now ponder what God has accomplished in Christ Jesus and Mary on my behalf in light of this particular mystery:

✳ I now pray to understand how the truth of this universal Mystery uniquely applies to my own Sacred Story:

✳ I examine my own life in light of how I have or have not lived up to the ideal to which the Mystery invites me to model:

✳ I close with a prayer of thanksgiving to Christ and Mary for walking the path of the Mystery in complete fidelity to the Father's will. I pray that I can be inspired by the Mystery's high ideal once again and that I too, can more faithfully live it in my own Sacred Story.

THE PRESENTATION OF THE CHILD JESUS

✳ I speak the mystery in my heart allowing its truth to shape my time of prayer.

✳ I now ponder what God has accomplished in Christ Jesus and Mary on my behalf in light of this particular mystery:

✳ I now pray to understand how the truth of this universal Mystery uniquely applies to my own Sacred Story:

✳ I examine my own life in light of how I have or have not lived up to the ideal to which the Mystery invites me to model:

✳ I close with a prayer of thanksgiving to Christ and Mary for walking the path of the Mystery in complete fidelity to the Father's will. I pray that I can be inspired by the Mystery's high ideal once again and that I too, can more faithfully live it in my own Sacred Story.

The Finding of Our Lord in the Temple

✳ I speak the mystery in my heart allowing its truth to shape my time of prayer.

✳ I now ponder what God has accomplished in Christ Jesus and Mary on my behalf in light of this particular mystery:

✳ I now pray to understand how the truth of this universal Mystery uniquely applies to my own Sacred Story:

✳ I examine my own life in light of how I have or have not lived up to the ideal to which the Mystery invites me to model:

✳ I close with a prayer of thanksgiving to Christ and Mary for walking the path of the Mystery in complete fidelity to the Father's will. I pray that I can be inspired by the Mystery's high ideal once again and that I too, can more faithfully live it in my own Sacred Story.

The Agony in the Garden

✳ I speak the mystery in my heart allowing its truth to shape my time of prayer.

✳ I now ponder what God has accomplished in Christ Jesus and Mary on my behalf in light of this particular mystery:

✳ I now pray to understand how the truth of this universal Mystery uniquely applies to my own Sacred Story:

✳ I examine my own life in light of how I have or have not lived up to the ideal to which the Mystery invites me to model:

✳ I close with a prayer of thanksgiving to Christ and Mary for walking the path of the Mystery in complete fidelity to the Father's will. I pray that I can be inspired by the Mystery's high ideal once again and that I too, can more faithfully live it in my own Sacred Story.

THE SCOURGING AT THE PILLAR

✳ I speak the mystery in my heart allowing its truth to shape my time of prayer.

✳ I now ponder what God has accomplished in Christ Jesus and Mary on my behalf in light of this particular mystery:

✳ I now pray to understand how the truth of this universal Mystery uniquely applies to my own Sacred Story:

✳ I examine my own life in light of how I have or have not lived up to the ideal to which the Mystery invites me to model:

✳ I close with a prayer of thanksgiving to Christ and Mary for walking the path of the Mystery in complete fidelity to the Father's will. I pray that I can be inspired by the Mystery's high ideal once again and that I too, can more faithfully live it in my own Sacred Story.

The Crowning with Thorns

✳ I speak the mystery in my heart allowing its truth to shape my time of prayer.

✳ I now ponder what God has accomplished in Christ Jesus and Mary on my behalf in light of this particular mystery:

✳ I now pray to understand how the truth of this universal Mystery uniquely applies to my own Sacred Story:

✳ I examine my own life in light of how I have or have not lived up to the ideal to which the Mystery invites me to model:

✳ I close with a prayer of thanksgiving to Christ and Mary for walking the path of the Mystery in complete fidelity to the Father's will. I pray that I can be inspired by the Mystery's high ideal once again and that I too, can more faithfully live it in my own Sacred Story.

THE CARRYING OF THE CROSS

✳ I speak the mystery in my heart allowing its truth to shape my time of prayer.

✳ I now ponder what God has accomplished in Christ Jesus and Mary on my behalf in light of this particular mystery:

✳ I now pray to understand how the truth of this universal Mystery uniquely applies to my own Sacred Story:

✳ I examine my own life in light of how I have or have not lived up to the ideal to which the Mystery invites me to model:

✳ I close with a prayer of thanksgiving to Christ and Mary for walking the path of the Mystery in complete fidelity to the Father's will. I pray that I can be inspired by the Mystery's high ideal once again and that I too, can more faithfully live it in my own Sacred Story.

THE CRUCIFIXION AND DEATH OF THE LORD

✳ I speak the mystery in my heart allowing its truth to shape my time of prayer.

✳ I now ponder what God has accomplished in Christ Jesus and Mary on my behalf in light of this particular mystery:

✳ I now pray to understand how the truth of this universal Mystery uniquely applies to my own Sacred Story:

✳ I examine my own life in light of how I have or have not lived up to the ideal to which the Mystery invites me to model:

✳ I close with a prayer of thanksgiving to Christ and Mary for walking the path of the Mystery in complete fidelity to the Father's will. I pray that I can be inspired by the Mystery's high ideal once again and that I too, can more faithfully live it in my own Sacred Story.

THE RESURRECTION

✳ I speak the mystery in my heart allowing its truth to shape my time of prayer.

✳ I now ponder what God has accomplished in Christ Jesus and Mary on my behalf in light of this particular mystery:

✳ I now pray to understand how the truth of this universal Mystery uniquely applies to my own Sacred Story:

✳ I examine my own life in light of how I have or have not lived up to the ideal to which the Mystery invites me to model:

✳ I close with a prayer of thanksgiving to Christ and Mary for walking the path of the Mystery in complete fidelity to the Father's will. I pray that I can be inspired by the Mystery's high ideal once again and that I too, can more faithfully live it in my own Sacred Story.

THE ASCENSION

✳ I speak the mystery in my heart allowing its truth to shape my time of prayer.

✳ I now ponder what God has accomplished in Christ Jesus and Mary on my behalf in light of this particular mystery:

✳ I now pray to understand how the truth of this universal Mystery uniquely applies to my own Sacred Story:

✳ I examine my own life in light of how I have or have not lived up to the ideal to which the Mystery invites me to model:

✳ I close with a prayer of thanksgiving to Christ and Mary for walking the path of the Mystery in complete fidelity to the Father's will. I pray that I can be inspired by the Mystery's high ideal once again and that I too, can more faithfully live it in my own Sacred Story.

THE DESCENT OF THE HOLY SPIRIT

✻ I speak the mystery in my heart allowing its truth to shape my time of prayer.

✻ I now ponder what God has accomplished in Christ Jesus and Mary on my behalf in light of this particular mystery:

✻ I now pray to understand how the truth of this universal Mystery uniquely applies to my own Sacred Story:

✻ I examine my own life in light of how I have or have not lived up to the ideal to which the Mystery invites me to model:

✻ I close with a prayer of thanksgiving to Christ and Mary for walking the path of the Mystery in complete fidelity to the Father's will. I pray that I can be inspired by the Mystery's high ideal once again and that I too, can more faithfully live it in my own Sacred Story.

THE ASSUMPTION OF MARY

✳ I speak the mystery in my heart allowing its truth to shape my time of prayer.

✳ I now ponder what God has accomplished in Christ Jesus and Mary on my behalf in light of this particular mystery:

✳ I now pray to understand how the truth of this universal Mystery uniquely applies to my own Sacred Story:

✳ I examine my own life in light of how I have or have not lived up to the ideal to which the Mystery invites me to model:

✳ I close with a prayer of thanksgiving to Christ and Mary for walking the path of the Mystery in complete fidelity to the Father's will. I pray that I can be inspired by the Mystery's high ideal once again and that I too, can more faithfully live it in my own Sacred Story.

THE CORONATION OF MARY

✳ I speak the mystery in my heart allowing its truth to shape my time of prayer.

✳ I now ponder what God has accomplished in Christ Jesus and Mary on my behalf in light of this particular mystery:

✳ I now pray to understand how the truth of this universal Mystery uniquely applies to my own Sacred Story:

✳ I examine my own life in light of how I have or have not lived up to the ideal to which the Mystery invites me to model:

✳ I close with a prayer of thanksgiving to Christ and Mary for walking the path of the Mystery in complete fidelity to the Father's will. I pray that I can be inspired by the Mystery's high ideal once again and that I too, can more faithfully live it in my own Sacred Story.

THE BAPTISM IN THE JORDAN

✳ I speak the mystery in my heart allowing its truth to shape my time of prayer.

✳ I now ponder what God has accomplished in Christ Jesus and Mary on my behalf in light of this particular mystery:

✳ I now pray to understand how the truth of this universal Mystery uniquely applies to my own Sacred Story:

✳ I examine my own life in light of how I have or have not lived up to the ideal to which the Mystery invites me to model:

✳ I close with a prayer of thanksgiving to Christ and Mary for walking the path of the Mystery in complete fidelity to the Father's will. I pray that I can be inspired by the Mystery's high ideal once again and that I too, can more faithfully live it in my own Sacred Story.

THE WEDDING AT CANA

✳ I speak the mystery in my heart allowing its truth to shape my time of prayer.

✳ I now ponder what God has accomplished in Christ Jesus and Mary on my behalf in light of this particular mystery:

✳ I now pray to understand how the truth of this universal Mystery uniquely applies to my own Sacred Story:

✳ I examine my own life in light of how I have or have not lived up to the ideal to which the Mystery invites me to model:

✳ I close with a prayer of thanksgiving to Christ and Mary for walking the path of the Mystery in complete fidelity to the Father's will. I pray that I can be inspired by the Mystery's high ideal once again and that I too, can more faithfully live it in my own Sacred Story.

THE PROCLAMATION OF THE KINGDOM

✳ I speak the mystery in my heart allowing its truth to shape my time of prayer.

✳ I now ponder what God has accomplished in Christ Jesus and Mary on my behalf in light of this particular mystery:

✳ I now pray to understand how the truth of this universal Mystery uniquely applies to my own Sacred Story:

✳ I examine my own life in light of how I have or have not lived up to the ideal to which the Mystery invites me to model:

✳ I close with a prayer of thanksgiving to Christ and Mary for walking the path of the Mystery in complete fidelity to the Father's will. I pray that I can be inspired by the Mystery's high ideal once again and that I too, can more faithfully live it in my own Sacred Story.

THE TRANSFIGURATION

✳ I speak the mystery in my heart allowing its truth to shape my time of prayer.

✳ I now ponder what God has accomplished in Christ Jesus and Mary on my behalf in light of this particular mystery:

✳ I now pray to understand how the truth of this universal Mystery uniquely applies to my own Sacred Story:

✳ I examine my own life in light of how I have or have not lived up to the ideal to which the Mystery invites me to model:

✳ I close with a prayer of thanksgiving to Christ and Mary for walking the path of the Mystery in complete fidelity to the Father's will. I pray that I can be inspired by the Mystery's high ideal once again and that I too, can more faithfully live it in my own Sacred Story.

The Institution of the Eucharist

✳ I speak the mystery in my heart allowing its truth to shape my time of prayer.

✳ I now ponder what God has accomplished in Christ Jesus and Mary on my behalf in light of this particular mystery:

✳ I now pray to understand how the truth of this universal Mystery uniquely applies to my own Sacred Story:

✳ I examine my own life in light of how I have or have not lived up to the ideal to which the Mystery invites me to model:

✳ I close with a prayer of thanksgiving to Christ and Mary for walking the path of the Mystery in complete fidelity to the Father's will. I pray that I can be inspired by the Mystery's high ideal once again and that I too, can more faithfully live it in my own Sacred Story.

PAPAL MARIAN PRAYERS AND REFLECTIONS

From St. John XXIII

To

Pope Francis[13]

POPE FRANCIS

Prayer for Peace (8 June, 2014)

*Lord God of peace, hear our prayer!
We have tried so many times and over so many years to resolve our
conflicts by our own powers and by the force of our arms. How
many moments of hostility and darkness have we experienced; how
much blood has been shed; how many lives have been shattered;
how many hopes have been buried... But our efforts have been in
vain.*

*Now, Lord, come to our aid! Grant us peace, teach us peace; guide
our steps in the way of peace. Open our eyes and our hearts, and
give us the courage to say: "Never again war!"; "With war
everything is lost". Instill in our hearts the courage to take concrete
steps to achieve peace.
Lord, God of Abraham, God of the Prophets, God of Love, you
created us and you call us to live as brothers and sisters. Give us the
strength daily to be instruments of peace; enable us to see everyone
who crosses our path as our brother or sister. Make us sensitive to
the plea of our citizens who entreat us to turn our weapons of war
into implements of peace, our trepidation into confident trust, and
our quarreling into forgiveness.*

*Keep alive within us the flame of hope, so that with patience and
perseverance we may opt for dialogue and reconciliation. In this
way may peace triumph at last, and may the words "division",
"hatred" and "war" be banished from the heart of every man and
woman. Lord, defuse the violence of our tongues and our hands.
Renew our hearts and minds, so that the word which always brings*

us together will be "brother", and our way of life will always be that of: Shalom, Peace, Salaam!
Amen.

To the Holy Family for the Extraordinary Synod (29 December, 2013)

Jesus, Mary and Joseph,
in you we contemplate
the splendour of true love,
to you we turn with trust.
Holy Family of Nazareth,
grant that our families too
may be places of communion and prayer,
authentic schools of the Gospel
and small domestic Churches.
Holy Family of Nazareth,
may families never again
experience violence, rejection and division:
may all who have been hurt or scandalized
find ready comfort and healing.
Holy Family of Nazareth,
may the approaching Synod of Bishops
make us once more mindful
of the sacredness and inviolability of the family,
and its beauty in God's plan.
Jesus, Mary and Joseph,
graciously hear our prayer.
Prayer to the Immaculate (8 December, 2013)

Virgin most holy and immaculate,
to you, the honour of our people,

and the loving protector of our city,
do we turn with loving trust.

You are all-beautiful, O Mary!
In you there is no sin.

Awaken in all of us a renewed desire for holiness:
May the splendour of truth shine forth in our words,
the song of charity resound in our works,
purity and chastity abide in our hearts and bodies,
and the full beauty of the Gospel be evident in our lives.

You are all-beautiful, O Mary!
In you the Word of God became flesh.

Help us always to heed the Lord's voice:
May we never be indifferent to the cry of the poor,
or untouched by the sufferings of the sick and those in need;
may we be sensitive to the loneliness of the elderly and the
vulnerability of children,
and always love and cherish the life of every human being.
You are all-beautiful, O Mary!
In you is the fullness of joy born of life with God.
Help us never to forget the meaning of our earthly journey:
May the kindly light of faith illumine our days,
the comforting power of hope direct our steps,
the contagious warmth of love stir our hearts;
and may our gaze be fixed on God, in whom true joy is found.
You are all-beautiful, O Mary!
Hear our prayer, graciously hear our plea:
May the beauty of God's merciful love in Jesus abide in our hearts,
and may this divine beauty save us,
our city and the entire world. Amen.

Prayer to the Blessed Virgin Mary in the Apostolic Exhortation Evangelii Gaudium (24 November, 2013)

Mary, Virgin and Mother,
you who, moved by the Holy Spirit,
welcomed the word of life
in the depths of your humble faith:
as you gave yourself completely to the Eternal One,
help us to say our own "yes"
to the urgent call, as pressing as ever,
to proclaim the good news of Jesus.
Filled with Christ's presence,
you brought joy to John the Baptist,
making him exult in the womb of his mother.
Brimming over with joy,
you sang of the great things done by God.
Standing at the foot of the cross
with unyielding faith,
you received the joyful comfort of the resurrection,
and joined the disciples in awaiting the Spirit
so that the evangelizing Church might be born.
Obtain for us now a new ardour born of the resurrection,
that we may bring to all the Gospel of life
which triumphs over death.
Give us a holy courage to seek new paths,
that the gift of unfading beauty
may reach every man and woman.
Virgin of listening and contemplation,
Mother of love, Bride of the eternal wedding feast,
pray for the Church, whose pure icon you are,
that she may never be closed in on herself

or lose her passion for establishing God's kingdom.
Star of the new evangelization,
help us to bear radiant witness to communion,
service, ardent and generous faith,
justice and love of the poor,
that the joy of the Gospel
may reach to the ends of the earth,
illuminating even the fringes of our world.

Mother of the living Gospel,
wellspring of happiness for God's little ones,
Pray for us.
Amen. Alleluia!

Act of Entrustment to Mary, Blessed Virgin Mary of Fatima (13 October, 2013)

Blessed Virgin Mary of Fatima,
with renewed gratitude for your motherly presence
we join in the voice of all generations that call you blessed.
We celebrate in you the great works of God,
who never tires of lowering himself in mercy over humanity,
afflicted by evil and wounded by sin,
to heal and to save it.
Accept with the benevolence of a Mother
this act of entrustment that we make in faith today,
before this your image, beloved to us.
We are certain that each one of us is precious in your eyes
and that nothing in our hearts has estranged you.
May that we allow your sweet gaze
to reach us and the perpetual warmth of your smile.

Guard our life with your embrace:
bless and strengthen every desire for good;
give new life and nourishment to faith;
sustain and enlighten hope;
awaken and animate charity;
guide us all on the path to holiness.
Teach us your own special love for the little and the poor,
for the excluded and the suffering,
for sinners and the wounded of heart:
gather all people under you protection
and give us all to your beloved Son, our Lord Jesus.
Amen.

To Our Lady of Bonaria (22 September, 2013)

Mary, today we would like to say to you: Mary, give us the gift of your gaze! Your gaze leads us to God, your gaze is a gift of the good Father that attends to us at every turn of our journey, it is a gift of Jesus Christ on the cross, who takes our sufferings, our toil, our sin upon himself. And to encounter this Father full of love we say today: Mary, give us the gift of your gaze! Let us say it all together: "Mary, give us the gift of your gaze! Mary, give us the gift of your gaze!"

Mother, give us the gift of your gaze! Let no one hide it! May our filial heart know how to defend it from the many words that cause illusions; from those who have a covetous gaze wanting an easy life, of promises that they cannot keep. Let them not rob us of Mary's gaze, which is full of tenderness, that gives us strength, that makes us solidary with each other. Let us all say together: Mother, give us the gift of your gaze! Mother, give us the gift of your gaze! Mother, give us the gift of your gaze!

Act of Consecration to Our Lady of Aparecida
(24 July, 2013)

Mary Most Holy by the merits of Our Lord Jesus Christ, in your beloved image of Aparecida, spread infinite favours over all Brazil.

I, unworthy to be counted among your sons and daughters but full of desire to share in the blessings of your mercy, lie prostrate at your feet. To you I consecrate my intentions, that they may ever dwell on the love that you merit; to you I consecrate my tongue that it may ever praise you and spread your devotion; to you I consecrate my heart, that, after God, I may love you above all things.

Receive me, incomparable Queen, you whom Christ Crucified gave to us as Mother, and count me among your blessed sons and daughters; take me under your protection; come to my aid in all my needs, both spiritual and temporal, and above all at the hour of my death.

Bless me, heavenly helper, and through your powerful intercession, give me strength in my weakness, so that, by serving you faithfully in this life, I may praise you, love you and give you thanks in heaven, for all eternity. Let it be!

Prayer to the Lord (25 July, 2013)
APOSTOLIC JOURNEY TO RIO DE JANEIRO
ON THE OCCASION OF
THE XXVIII WORLD YOUTH DAY

Lord you left your Mother in our midst that she might accompany us. May she take care of us and protect us on our journey, in our hearts, in our faith. May she make us disciples like herself,

missionaries like herself. May she teach us to go out onto the streets.
May she teach us to step outside ourselves.
We bless this image, Lord, which will travel round the country.
May she, by her meekness, by her peace, show us the way.
Lord, you are a scandal. You are a scandal: the scandal of the Cross.
A Cross which is humility, meekness; a Cross that speaks to us of
God's closeness. We bless this image of the Cross that will travel
round the country.

Prayer to Mary, Mother of the Church and of our Faith (29 June, 2013)[14]

Let us turn in prayer to Mary,
Mother of the Church and Mother of our faith.
Mother, help our faith!
Open our ears to hear God's word and to recognize his voice and
call. Awaken in us a desire to follow in his footsteps, to go forth
from our own land and to receive his promise.
Help us to be touched by his love, that we may touch him in faith.
Help us to entrust ourselves fully to him and to believe in his love,
especially at times of trial, beneath the shadow of the cross, when
our faith is called to mature.
Sow in our faith the joy of the Risen One.
Remind us that those who believe are never alone.
Teach us to see all things with the eyes of Jesus, that he may be light
for our path. And may this light of faith always increase in us, until
the dawn of that undying day which is
Christ himself, your Son, our Lord!

Prayer to Mary, Woman of Listening (31 May, 2013)[15]

Mary, woman of listening, open our ears; grant us to know how to listen to the word of your Son Jesus among the thousands of words of this world; grant that we may listen to the reality in which we live, to every person we encounter, especially those who are poor, in need, in hardship.

Mary, woman of decision, illuminate our mind and our heart, so that we may obey, unhesitating, the word of your Son Jesus; give us the courage to decide, not to let ourselves be dragged along, letting others direct our life.

Mary, woman of action, obtain that our hands and feet move "with haste" toward others, to bring them the charity and love of your Son Jesus, to bring the light of the Gospel to the world, as you did. Amen.

Prayer to Mary, Mother of Silence (23 May, 2013)[16]

Mother of silence, who watches over the mystery of God, Save us from the idolatry of the present time, to which those who forget are condemned. Purify the eyes of Pastors with the eye-wash of memory: Take us back to the freshness of the origins, for a prayerful, penitent Church. Mother of the beauty that blossoms from faithfulness to daily work, Lift us from the torpor of laziness, pettiness, and defeatism. Clothe Pastors in the compassion that unifies, that makes whole; let us discover the joy of a humble, brotherly, serving Church. Mother of tenderness who envelops us in patience and mercy, Help us burn away the sadness, impatience and rigidity of those who do not know what it means to belong. Intercede with your Son to obtain that our hands, our feet, our

hearts be agile: let us build the Church with the Truth of love.
Mother, we shall be the People of God,
pilgrims bound for the Kingdom.
Amen.

POPE BENEDICT XVI

Spe Salvi (November 30, 2007)
Mary, Star of Hope

With a hymn composed in the eighth or ninth century, thus for over a thousand years, the Church has greeted Mary, the Mother of God, as "Star of the Sea": Ave Maris Stella. Human life is a journey. Towards what destination? How do we find the way? Life is like a voyage on the sea of history, often dark and stormy, a voyage in which we watch for the stars that indicate the route. The true stars of our life are the people who have lived good lives. They are lights of hope. Certainly, Jesus Christ is the true light, the sun that has risen above all the shadows of history. But to reach him we also need lights close by—people who shine with his light and so guide us along our way. Who more than Mary could be a star of hope for us? With her "yes" she opened the door of our world to God himself; she became the living Ark of the Covenant, in whom God took flesh, became one of us, and pitched his tent among us (cf. Jn 1:14).

So we cry to her: Holy Mary, you belonged to the humble and great souls of Israel who, like Simeon, were "looking for the consolation of Israel" (Lk 2:25) and hoping, like Anna, "for the redemption of Jerusalem" (Lk 2:38). Your life was thoroughly imbued with the sacred scriptures of Israel which spoke of hope, of the promise made to Abraham and his descendants (Lk 1:55). In this way we can appreciate the holy fear that overcame you when the angel of the Lord appeared to you and told you that you would give birth to the One who was the hope of Israel, the One awaited by the world. Through you, through your "yes", the hope of the ages became reality, entering this world and its history.

You bowed low before the greatness of this task and gave your consent: "Behold, I am the handmaid of the Lord; let it be to me according to your word" (Lk 1:38). When you hastened with holy joy across the mountains of Judea to see your cousin Elizabeth, you became the image of the Church to come, which carries the hope of the world in her womb across the mountains of history.

But alongside the joy which, with your Magnificat, you proclaimed in word and song for all the centuries to hear, you also knew the dark sayings of the prophets about the suffering of the servant of God in this world. Shining over his birth in the stable at Bethlehem, there were angels in splendour who brought the good news to the shepherds, but at the same time the lowliness of God in this world was all too palpable. The old man Simeon spoke to you of the sword which would pierce your soul (cf. Lk 2:35), of the sign of contradiction that your Son would be in this world. Then, when Jesus began his public ministry, you had to step aside, so that a new family could grow, the family which it was his mission to establish and which would be made up of those who heard his word and kept it (Lk 11:27f).

Notwithstanding the great joy that marked the beginning of Jesus's ministry, in the synagogue of Nazareth you must already have experienced the truth of the saying about the "sign of contradiction" (cf. Lk 4:28ff). In this way you saw the growing power of hostility and rejection which built up around Jesus until the hour of the Cross, when you had to look upon the Saviour of the world, the heir of David, the Son of God dying like a failure, exposed to mockery, between criminals. Then you received the word of Jesus: "Woman, behold, your Son!" (Jn 19:26).

From the Cross you received a new mission. From the Cross you became a mother in a new way: the mother of all those who believe in your Son Jesus and wish to follow him. The sword of sorrow pierced your heart. Did hope die? Did the world remain definitively without light, and life without purpose? At that moment, deep down, you probably listened again to the word spoken by the angel in answer to your fear at the time of the Annunciation: "Do not be afraid, Mary!" (Lk 1:30). How many times had the Lord, your Son, said the same thing to his disciples: do not be afraid! In your heart, you heard this word again during the night of Golgotha. Before the hour of his betrayal he had said to his disciples: "Be of good cheer, I have overcome the world" (Jn 16:33). "Let not your hearts be troubled, neither let them be afraid" (Jn 14:27).

"Do not be afraid, Mary!" In that hour at Nazareth the angel had also said to you: "Of his kingdom there will be no end" (Lk 1:33). Could it have ended before it began? No, at the foot of the Cross, on the strength of Jesus's own word, you became the mother of believers. In this faith, which even in the darkness of Holy Saturday bore the certitude of hope, you made your way towards Easter morning.

The joy of the Resurrection touched your heart and united you in a new way to the disciples, destined to become the family of Jesus through faith. In this way you were in the midst of the community of believers, who in the days following the Ascension prayed with one voice for the gift of the Holy Spirit (cf. Acts 1:14) and then received that gift on the day of Pentecost.

The "Kingdom" of Jesus was not as might have been imagined. It began in that hour, and of this "Kingdom" there will be no end. Thus you remain in the midst of the disciples as their Mother, as the Mother of hope. Holy Mary, Mother of God, our Mother, teach us to believe, to hope, to love with you. Show us the way to his Kingdom! Star of the Sea, shine upon us and guide us on our way!

Deus Caritas Est (December 25, 2005)

Holy Mary, Mother of God, you have given the world its true light,
Jesus, your Son – the Son of God.
You abandoned yourself completely to God's call
and thus became a wellspring of the goodness which flows forth
from him. Show us Jesus. Lead us to him.
Teach us to know and love him, so that we too can become
capable of true love and be fountains of living water
in the midst of a thirsting world.

ST. POPE JOHN PAUL II

Fides et Ratio (14 September, 1998)

May Mary, Seat of Wisdom, be a sure haven for all who devote their lives to the search for wisdom. May their journey into wisdom, sure and final goal of all true knowing, be freed of every hindrance by the intercession of the one who, in giving birth to the Truth and treasuring it in her heart, has shared it forever with all the world.

Evangelium Vitae (25 March, 1995)

O Mary,
bright dawn of the new world,
Mother of the living,
to you do we entrust the cause of life
Look down, O Mother,
upon the vast numbers
of babies not allowed to be born,
of the poor whose lives are made difficult,
of men and women
who are victims of brutal violence,
of the elderly and the sick killed
by indifference or out of misguided mercy.

Grant that all who believe in your Son
may proclaim the Gospel of life
with honesty and love
to the people of our time.

Obtain for them the grace
to accept that Gospel
as a gift ever new,
the joy of celebrating it with gratitude
throughout their lives
and the courage to bear witness to it
resolutely, in order to build,
together with all people of good will,
the civilization of truth and love,
to the praise and glory of God,
the Creator and lover of life.

Veritatis Splendor (6 August, 1993)

O Mary, Mother of Mercy,
watch over all people, that the Cross of Christ
may not be emptied of its power, that man may not stray
from the path of the good or become blind to sin,
but may put his hope ever more fully in God
who is "rich in mercy" (Eph 2:4).
May he carry out the good works prepared
by God beforehand (cf. Eph 2:10) and so live completely
"for the praise of his glory" (Eph 1:12).

Centesimus Annus (1 May, 1991)

Mary, the Mother of the Redeemer, constantly remained beside
Christ in his journey towards the human family and in its midst,
and she goes before the Church on the pilgrimage of faith. May her
maternal intercession accompany humanity towards the next
Millennium, in fidelity to him who "is the same yesterday and

today and for ever" (cf. Heb 13:8), Jesus Christ our Lord, in whose name I cordially impart my blessing to all.

Redemptoris Missio (7 December, 1990)

To "Mary's mediation, wholly oriented toward Christ and tending to the revelation of his salvific power," I entrust the Church and, in particular, those who commit themselves to carrying out the missionary mandate in today's world. As Christ sent forth his apostles in the name of the Father and of the Son and of the Holy Spirit, so too, renewing that same mandate, I extend to all of you my apostolic blessing, in the name of the same Most Holy Trinity. Amen.

Sollicitudo Rei Socialis (30 December, 1987)

Before the Most Blessed Trinity, I entrust to Mary all that I have written in this Encyclical, and I invite all to reflect and actively commit themselves to promoting the true development of peoples, as the prayer of the Mass for this intention states so well: "Father, you have given all peoples one common origin, and your will is to gather them as one family in yourself. Fill the hearts of all with the fire of your love, and the desire to ensure justice for all their brothers and sisters. By sharing the good things you give us, may we secure justice and equality for every human being, an end to all division and a human society built on love and peace." This, in conclusion, is what I ask in the name of all my brothers and sisters, to whom I send a special blessing as a sign of greeting and good wishes.

BLESSED POPE PAUL VI

Christi Matri (15 September, 1966)
An Appeal to Mary

Look down with maternal clemency, Most Blessed Virgin, upon all your children. Consider the anxiety of bishops who fear that their flocks will be tormented by a terrible storm of evils. Heed the anguish of so many people, fathers and mothers of families who are uncertain about their future and beset by hardships and cares. Soothe the minds of those at war and inspire them with "thoughts of peace." Through your intercession, may God, the avenger of injuries, turn to mercy. May He give back to nations the tranquility they seek and bring them to a lasting age of genuine prosperity.

With confidence that the exalted Mother of God will graciously hear Our humble prayer, We lovingly impart the apostolic blessing to you, venerable brethren, and to the clergy and people committed to your care.

Mysterium Fidei (September 3, 1965)
A Final Prayer

May the most blessed Virgin Mary, from whom Christ the Lord took the flesh that "is contained, offered, received" in this Sacrament under the appearances of bread and wine, and may all the saints of God and especially those who were more inflamed with ardent devotion toward the divine Eucharist, intercede with the Father of mercies so that this common belief in the Eucharist and devotion to it may give rise among all Christians to a perfect unity of communion that will continue to flourish. Lingering in Our mind are the words of the holy martyr Ignatius warning the Philadelphians against the evil of divisions and schisms, the remedy for which is to be found in the Eucharist. "Strive then," he says, "to make use of one single thanksgiving. For there is only one flesh of Our Lord Jesus Christ, and only one chalice unto the union of His blood, only one altar, only one bishop . . ."

Fortified by the most consoling hope of blessings that will accrue to the whole Church and to the whole world from an increase in devotion to the Eucharist, as a pledge of heavenly blessings We lovingly impart Our apostolic blessings to you, Venerable Brothers, and to the priests, religious and all who are helping you, as well as to all the faithful entrusted to your care.

Mense Maio (29 April, 1965)
Plea for Mary's Help

May she who experienced the cares and hardships of earthly life, the weariness of daily toil, the hardships and trials of poverty, and the sorrows of Calvary, come to aid the needs of the Church and the human race. May she graciously lend an ear to the devout pleas of those all over the world who beg her for peace. May she enlighten the minds of those who rule nations. And finally, may she prevail on God, who rules the winds and storms, to calm the tempests in men's warring hearts and grant us peace in our day. What we seek is true peace grounded on the sturdy foundations of justice and love—on a justice which recognizes the legitimate rights of the weak as well as those of the strong; on a love which keeps men from falling into error through excessive concern for their own interests. Thus each person's rights may be safeguarded without the rights of others being forgotten or violated.

ST. POPE JOHN XXIII

Princeps Pastorum (November 28, 1959)

From the bottom of Our heart, We call down upon the missions the worthy protection of their patrons and martyrs, and, first and foremost, the intercession of Mary, Mother and Queen of the Missions. With the greatest affection We impart to each one of you, Venerable Brethren, and to all those who in any way contribute to the propagation of God's kingdom, Our Apostolic Blessing. May it be a token and a pledge of the supernatural favors of the Eternal Father, who appeared to the world through His Son, the Savior of mankind, and may it kindle and multiply missionary zeal in the hearts of all.

HAIL, HOLY QUEEN[17]

Hail, holy Queen, Mother of Mercy,
our life, our sweetness and our hope.
To thee do we cry, poor banished children of Eve;
To thee do we send forth our sighs,
Mourning and weeping in this vale of tears.
Turn then, most gracious advocate,
Thine eyes of mercy toward us; and after this our exile,
Show unto us the blessed fruit of thy womb, Jesus.
O clement, O loving,
O sweet Virgin Mary.
Pray for us O holy Mother of God,
That we may be made worthy
of the promises of Christ, thy Son.
Let us pray:
Almighty, everlasting God, who by the co-operation of the Holy
Spirit didst prepare the body and soul of the glorious Virgin-Mother
Mary to become a dwelling-place meet for thy Son: grant that as we
rejoice in her commemoration; so by her fervent intercession we may
be delivered from present evils and from everlasting death.

Through the same Christ our Lord. Amen!

AFTERWORD

O VIRGIN, BY WHOSE BLESSING
ALL NATURE IS BLESSED!

Blessed Lady, sky and stars, earth and rivers, day and night – everything that is subject to the power or use of man – rejoice that through you they are in some sense restored to their lost beauty and are endowed with inexpressible new grace. All creatures were dead, as it were, useless for men or for the praise of God, who made them. The world, contrary to its true destiny, was corrupted and tainted by the acts of men who served idols. Now all creation has been restored to life and rejoices that it is controlled and given splendour by men who believe in God.

The universe rejoices with new and indefinable loveliness. Not only does it feel the unseen presence of God himself, its Creator, it sees him openly, working and making it holy. These great blessings spring from the blessed fruit of Mary's womb.

Through the fullness of the grace that was given you, dead things rejoice in their freedom, and those in heaven are glad to be made new. Through the Son who was the glorious fruit of your virgin womb, just souls who died before his life-giving death rejoice as they are freed from captivity, and the angels are glad at the restoration of their shattered domain.

Lady, full and overflowing with grace, all creation receives new life from your abundance. Virgin, blessed above all creatures, through your blessing all creation is blessed, not only creation from its Creator, but the Creator himself has been blessed by creation.

To Mary God gave his only-begotten Son, whom he loved as himself. Through Mary God made himself a Son, not different but the same, by nature Son of God and Son of Mary. The whole universe was created by God, and God was born of Mary. God created all things, and Mary gave birth to God. The God who made all things gave himself form through Mary, and thus he made his own creation. He who could create all things from nothing would not remake his ruined creation without Mary.

God, then, is the Father of the created world and Mary the mother of the re-created world. God is the Father by whom all things were given life, and Mary the mother through whom all things were given new life. For God begot the Son, through whom all things were made, and Mary gave birth to him as the Saviour of the world. Without God's Son, nothing could exist; without Mary's Son, nothing could be redeemed.

Truly the Lord is with you, to whom the Lord granted that all nature should owe as much to you as to himself.

St Anselm, Bishop[18]

ABOUT THE AUTHOR

Fr. William Watson, S.J., D. Min., has spent over thirty years developing Ignatian programs and retreats. Fr. Watson has served as: Director of Retreat Programs at Georgetown University; Vice President for Mission at Gonzaga University; and Provincial Assistant for International Ministries for the Oregon Province of the Society of Jesus. He holds Masters Degrees in Divinity and Pastoral Studies, respectively (1986; Weston Jesuit School of Theology, Cambridge Massachusetts). He received his Doctor of Ministry degree in 2009 from The Catholic University of America (Washington D.C.).

In the spring of 2011 Fr. Watson launched the non-profit Sacred Story Institute, to bring Ignatian Spirituality to Catholics of all ages and walks of life. The Sacred Story Institute is promoting third millennium evangelization for the Society of Jesus and the Church by using the time-tested *Examination of Conscience* of St. Ignatius.

SACRED STORY PRESS
SEATTLE, WASHINGTON, USA
www.sacredstorypress.com

Sacred Story Press explores dynamic new dimensions of classic Ignatian spirituality, based on St. Ignatius' Conscience Examen in the *Sacred Story* prayer method pioneered by Fr. Bill Watson, S.J. We are creating a new class of spiritual resources. Our publications are research-based, authentic to the Catholic Tradition and designed to help individuals achieve integrated, spiritual growth and holiness of life.

We Request Your Feedback

The Sacred Story Institute welcomes feedback on all our publications. Contact us via email or letter. Give us ideas, suggestions and inspirations for how to make better resources for Catholics and Christians of all ages and walks of life.

FOR BULK ORDERS AND GROUP DISCOUNTS,
CONTACT US:
ADMIN-TEAM@SACREDSTORY.NET
SACRED STORY INSTITUTE & SACRED STORY PRESS
1401 E. JEFFERSON SUITE 405
SEATTLE, WASHINGTON, 98122

NOTES

[1] Pope John Paul II: *Rosarium Virginis Mariae: 2002,* ¶29.

[2] The Pope has written the preface to the Italian edition of a book on Marian prayer written by his secretary, Fr. Yoannia Lahzi Gaid. "The Rosary is a prayer that always accompanies me; it is also the prayer of the ordinary people and the saints … it a prayer from my heart." These words, handwritten by the Pope himself and dated 13 May 2014, are the preface to the book *"Il Rosario. Preghiera del cuore"* ("The Rosary: A prayer from the heart", Shalom Editions, pp. 210), written by the Coptic Catholic priest Yoannis Lahzi Gaid who has been working in the Pope's personal secretariat for about a month now. Reflecting over the first year of Francis' pontificate, Mgr. Alfred Xuereb, the Pope's former secretary, told Vatican Radio: "Pope Francis "does not waste a minute! He works tirelessly and, when he feels the need to take a moment's pause, he closes his eyes and does nothing: he simply sits and prays the Rosary. He prays at least three Rosaries a day I think. "This helps me unwind" he told me. Then he sets to work again."
http://vaticaninsider.lastampa.it/en/the-vatican/detail/articolo/francesco-francis-francisco-rosario-36247/

[3] "The Church begins there," he said, "in the heart of the Father, who had this idea . . . of love. So this love story began, a story that has gone on for so long, and is not yet ended. We, the women and men of the Church, we are in the middle of a love story: each of us is a link in this chain of love. And if we do not understand this, we have understood nothing of what the Church is." "But how does it increase?" Pope Francis asked himself. "Jesus said simply: like the mustard seed, it grows like yeast in the flour, without noise." General Audience of Pope Francis, 4-24-13:
http://vaticaninsider.lastampa.it/en/the-vatican/detail/articolo/papa-el-papa-pope-ior-chiesa-iglesia-church-24293/

[4] 1) To contribute effectively to the implementation of the Second Vatican Council;
2) To confront with all our forces the problem of atheism and cooperate in that profound renewal of the Church needed in a secularized age;
3) To better adapt our traditional apostolates to the different spiritual necessities of today: the renewal of Christian life, the education of youth, the formation of the clergy, the study of philosophy and theology, research into humanistic and scientific cultures, and missionary evangelization;
4) To pay particular attention to ecumenism, interreligious dialogue, and the task of authentic inculturation;

5) In a manner consonant with our priestly and religious Institute and within the Church's evangelizing action, to promote the justice "connected with peace, which is the aspiration of all peoples";
6) To foster the vigorous impulse toward missionary work and church union and to serve our prophetic mission to promote the new evangelization. *Constitutions of the Society of Jesus and Their Complimentary Norms.* Edited by John W. Padberg, SJ. St. Louis: Institute of Jesuit Sources, 277.

[5] As you well know because you have so often made the meditation "of the Two Standards" in the Spiritual Exercises under the guidance of St Ignatius, our world is the stage of a battle between good and evil, with powerful negative forces at work, which cause those dramatic situations of spiritual and material subjection of our contemporaries against which you have repeatedly declared your wish to combat, working for the service of the faith and the promotion of justice. These forces show themselves today in many forms, but with particular evidence through cultural tendencies that often become dominating, such as subjectivism, relativism, hedonism, practical materialism. This is why I have asked you to renew your interest in the promotion and defence of the Catholic doctrine "particularly in the neuralgic points strongly attacked today by secular culture", some of which I have mentioned in my letter. The issues, constantly discussed and questioned today, of the salvation in Christ of all human beings, of sexual morality, the marriage and the family, must be deepened and illumined in the context of contemporary reality, but keeping the harmony with the Magisterium, which avoids creating confusion and bewilderment among the People of God.
Selections from the February 21 2008 Address of His Holiness Benedict the Sixteenth to the 35th General Congregation of the Society of Jesus. Padberg, John: *Jesuit Life and Mission Today* (The Institute of Jesuit Sources: St. Louis, 2001 p. 824.

[6] http://sacredstory.net

[7] "And Pope John Paul II further commented: "The sacred deposit of God's word, handed on by the Church, is the joy and strength of our people's lives. It is the only pastoral solution to the many problems of our day." At this point, I would like to call your attention to the words the then-Cardinal Wojtyla is reported to have given in an address during the Eucharistic Congress in 1976 for the Bicentennial celebration of the signing of the Declaration of independence. it seems to be so profoundly prophetic:

"We are now standing in the face of the greatest historical confrontation humanity has ever experienced. I do not think that the wide circle of the American Society, or the whole wide circle of the Christian Community realize this fully. We are now facing the final confrontation between the Church and the anti-church, between the gospel and the anti-gospel, between Christ and the antichrist. The confrontation lies within the plans of Divine Providence. It is, therefore, in God's Plan, and it must be a trial which the Church must take up, and face courageously..."

These words that the then-Cardinal Wojtyla made his own appear to be inspired from the Diary of Saint Faustina Kowalska, who greatly influenced his spirituality. As Pope John Paul II, he proclaimed this Religious Sister a saint during the Jubilee Year of 2000. He died during Vespers of the feast of Divine Mercy, the feast which was inspired by Saint Faustina.

I view the above-quoted words of the Popes, John XXIII, Paul VI, and John Paul II, impressed clearly upon the history of the Church, as a call to attentiveness, watchfulness and preparedness for whatever proclaiming the Gospel may mean for us as successors of the Apostles, who were called to give radical witness to their faith in Jesus Christ." *Selections from the Address Of Archbishop Carlo Maria Viganò, Apostolic Nuncio To The United States USCCB Fall General Assembly*, Baltimore, Maryland November 11, 2013
http://www.usccb.org/about/leadership/usccb-general-assembly/2013-november-meeting/nuncio-address-2013.cfm

[8] See: *My Path to Peace and Justice*, from Fortkamp Publishing Company, (1996).

[9] Preamble 1: The first preamble is to recall the narrative of the subject to be contemplated, in this case how the three Divine Persons were looking at all the flatness or roundness of the whole world filled with people, and how the decision was taken in Their eternity, as They saw them all going down into hell, that the second Person would become human to save the human race. Thus when the 'the fullness of time' came They send the angel Gabriel to Our Lady [Exx. 262].

Preamble 2: The composition, seeing the place, which here will be to see the great extent of the round earth with it many different races; then, in the dame way, see the particular house of Our Lady and its rooms in the town of Nazareth in the province of Galilee.

Preamble 3: I ask for what I want: here I ask for interior knowledge of the Lord who became human for me so that I may better love and follow Him.
Point 1: This is to see the various kinds of persons: first, those on the face of the earth, in all their diversity of dress and appearance, some white and some black, some in peace and others at war, some weeping and others laughing, some healthy, others sick, some being born and others dying, etc.; second, I see and consider the three divine Persons, as though They are on the royal throne of their Divine

Majesty, how They look down on the whole round world and on all its peoples living in such great blindness, and dying and going down into hell; third, I see Our Lady and the Angel who greets her. And I should reflect in order to draw profit from such a sight." *St. Ignatius of Loyola: Personal Writings*: ed. Joseph Munitiz, Philip Endean (London, 1996), p 305.

[10] "Late have I loved you, O beauty ever ancient, ever new. Late have I loved you. You have called to me, and have called out, and have shattered my deafness. You have blazed forth with light and have put my blindness to flight! You have sent forth fragrance, and I have drawn in my breath, and I pant after you. I have tasted you, and I hunger and thirst after you. You have touched me, and I have burned for your peace." This famous excerpt from the Confessions of St. Augustine (Lib. 7, 10, 18; 10, 27: CSEL 33, 157-163, 255) is used in the Roman Office of Readings for the Feast of Saint Augustine on August 28th.

[11] Here is how I have framed the classic Examen for our *Sacred Story* prayer:

SACRED STORY PRAYER MEDITATIONS

Pray the whole 15-minute Sacred Story prayer once or twice daily and consciously repeat to Christ Jesus the five-word refrain whenever you are in the grip of fear, anxiety, grief or sins, addictions and destructive compulsions.

CREATION- I believe God created everything in love and for love; I ask for heart-felt knowledge of God's love for me, and for gratitude for the general and particular graces of this day.

PRESENCE- I believe God is present in each moment and event of my life, and I ask for the grace to awaken, see and feel where and how, especially in this present moment.

MEMORY- I believe every violation of love committed by me and against me is in my memory, and I ask God to reveal them to me, especially those that have manifested themselves today, so I can be healed.

MERCY- I believe that forgiveness is the only path to healing and illumination. I beg for the grace of forgiveness, and the grace to forgive, especially for the general and particular failures of this day, and from my past.

ETERNITY- I believe the grace of forgiveness opens my heart, making my every thought, word and deed bear fruit that endures to eternity. I ask that everything in my life serve Christ's Great Work of Reconciliation.

[12] In October 2002, the month of the Holy Rosary, Saint John Paul II, issued a special apostolic letter in which he announced the creation of a new set of Mysteries to be used in praying the Rosary. He states: "The Rosary clearly belongs to the kind of veneration of the Mother of God described by the Second Vatican Council: a devotion directed to the Christological center of the Christian faith, in such a way that when the Mother is honored, the Son...is duly known, loved and glorified." The new Mysteries center around decisive events in the life of Christ. And he called them "The Mysteries of Light" because Christ in his public life manifests himself as the "Mystery of Light."

[13] All the Encyclicals can be found at the Vatican Website: http://www.vatican.va/holy_father/ Image of Our Lady of the Rosary from Jesuit Community Chapel, Seattle University, Photo by William Watson.

[14] Prayer to Mary at the conclusion of the Encyclical *Lumen Fidei* (29 June, 2013)

[15] Prayer to Mary at the conclusion of the recital of the Holy Rosary (Saint Peter's Square, 31 May, 2013)

[16] Prayer to Mary after the Profession of Faith with the Bishops of the Italian Episcopal Conference (23 May, 2013)

[17] A prayer of all the Popes and the entire People of God!

[18] This excerpt from a sermon of St. Anselm (Oratio 52; PL 158, 955-956) is used in the Roman Office of Readings for the Solemnity (Solemn Feast) of the Immaculate Conception on December 8 along with the accompanying biblical reading from Romans 5:12-20.

CPSIA information can be obtained
at www.ICGtesting.com
Printed in the USA
LVOW13s0955010818

585588LV00019B/237/P